Here's all the great literature in this grade level of *Celebrate Reading!*

Books A–D

The Deciding Factor

Learning What Matters

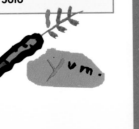

Featured Poet
Gary Soto

Book A Celebrate Reading!

A Volcano of Cheers

Chasing Your Goals

Book B Celebrate Reading!

The First Magnificent Web

Tales of the Imagination

Featured Poets
Jack Prelutsky
Lewis Carroll
Richard Armour
Eve Merriam

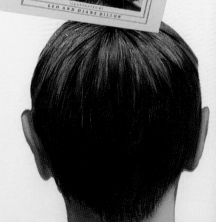

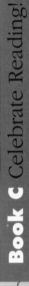

Book C Celebrate Reading!

A Better Time Slot

From There to Here

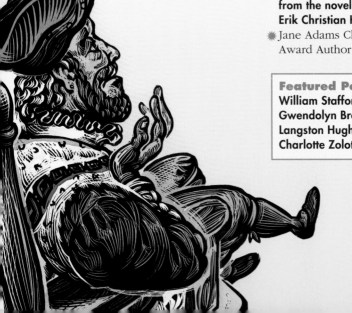

Trade Books Celebrate Reading!

The Grizzly
by Annabel and
Edgar Johnson

**Where the Lillies
Bloom**
by Vera and Bill Cleaver

The Master Puppeteer
by Katherine Paterson

**The Bread Sister of
Sinking Creek**
by Robin Moore

Maniac Magee
by Jerry Spinelli

Sweetwater
by Laurence Yep

It's Like This, Cat
by Emily Neville

Let the Hurricane Roar
by Rose Wilder Lane

THE FIRST MAGNIFICENT WEB

TALES OF THE IMAGINATION

TITLES IN THIS SET

Cover Artist
Although physics was Michael Paraskevas's first interest,
he says that eventually painting took over his life. Today
Paraskevas spends most of his hours in front of an easel
but admits that sometimes he would rather be seated
behind first base in any ballpark in the United States.

ISBN 0-673-80075-X

Acknowledgments appear on page 128.

5678910RRS9998979695

THE FIRST MAGNIFICENT WEB

TALES OF THE IMAGINATION

ScottForesman

A Division of HarperCollins*Publishers*

C O N T E N T S

STAGE VOICES

Nothing to Be Afraid Of

by Jan Mark

"Robin won't give you any trouble," said Auntie Lynn. "He's very quiet."

Anthea knew how quiet Robin was. At present he was sitting under the table, and until Auntie Lynn had mentioned his name, she had forgotten that he was there.

Auntie Lynn put an overnight bag on the armchair.

"There's plenty of clothes, so you won't need to do any washing, and there's a spare pair of pajamas in case—well, you know. In case . . . "

"Yes," said Mum firmly. "He'll be all right. I'll ring you tonight and let you know how he's getting along." She looked at the clock. "Now, hadn't *you* better be getting along?"

She saw Auntie Lynn to the front door and Anthea heard them saying good-bye to each other. Mum almost told Auntie Lynn to stop worrying and have a good time, which would have been a mistake because Auntie Lynn was going up north to a funeral.

Auntie Lynn was not really an aunt, but she had once been at school with Anthea's mum, and she was the kind of person who couldn't manage without a handle to her name; so Robin was not Anthea's cousin. Robin was not anything much, except four years old, and he looked a lot younger; probably because nothing ever happened to him. Auntie Lynn kept no pets that might give Robin germs, and never bought him toys that had sharp corners to dent him or wheels that could be swallowed. He wore knitted balaclava helmets and pompom hats in winter to protect his tender ears, and a knitted undershirt in summer in case he overheated himself and caught a chill from his own sweat.

"Perspiration," said Auntie Lynn.

His face was as pale and flat as a saucer of milk, and his eyes floated in it like drops of cod-liver oil. This was not so surprising, as he was full to the back teeth with cod-liver oil; also with extract of malt, concentrated orange juice, and calves'-foot jelly. When you picked him up you expected him to squelch, like a hot-water bottle full of half-set custard.

Anthea lifted the tablecloth and looked at him.

"Hello, Robin."

Robin stared at her with his flat eyes and went back to sucking his wooly doggy that had flat eyes also, of sewn-on felt, because glass ones might find their way into Robin's appendix and cause damage. Anthea wondered how long it would be before he noticed that his mother had gone. Probably he wouldn't, any more than he would notice when she came back.

Mum closed the front door and joined Anthea in looking under the table at Robin. Robin's mouth turned down at the corners, and Anthea hoped he would cry so that they could cuddle him. It seemed impolite to cuddle him before he needed it. Anthea was afraid to go any closer.

"What a little troll," said Mum sadly, lowering the tablecloth. "I suppose he'll come out when he's hungry."

Anthea doubted it.

Robin didn't want any lunch or any tea.

"Do you think he's pining?" said Mum. Anthea did not. Anthea had a nasty suspicion that he was like this all the time. He went to bed without making a fuss and fell asleep before the light was out, as if he were too bored to stay awake. Anthea left her bedroom door open, hoping that he would have a nightmare so that she could go in and comfort him, but Robin slept all night without a squeak, and woke in the morning as flat faced as before. Wall-eyed Doggy looked more excitable than Robin did.

"If only we had a proper garden," said Mum, as Robin went under the table again, leaving his breakfast eggs scattered round the plate. "He might run about."

Anthea thought that this was unlikely, and in any case they didn't have a proper garden, only a yard at the back and a stony strip in front, without a fence.

"Can I take him to the park?" said Anthea.

Mum looked doubtful. "Do you think he wants to go?"

"No," said Anthea, peering under the tablecloth. "I don't think he wants to do anything, but he can't sit there all day."

"I bet he can," said Mum. "Still, I don't think he should. All right, take him to the park, but keep quiet about it. I don't suppose Lynn thinks you're safe in traffic."

"He might tell her."

"Can he talk?"

Robin, still clutching wall-eyed Doggy, plodded beside her all the way to the park, without once trying to jam his head between the library railings or get run over by a bus.

"Hold my hand, Robin," Anthea said as they left the house, and he clung to her like a lamprey.

The park was not really a park at all; it was a garden. It did not even pretend to be a park, and the notice by the gate said KING STREET GARDENS, in case anyone tried to use it as a park. The grass was as green and as flat as the front-room carpet, but the front-room carpet had a path worn across it from the door to the fireplace, and here there were more notices that said KEEP OFF THE GRASS, so that the gritty white paths went obediently round the edge, under the orderly trees that stood in a row like the queue outside a fish shop. There were bushes in each corner and one shelter with a bench in it. Here and there brown holes in the grass, full of raked earth, waited for next year's flowers, but there were no flowers now, and the bench had been taken out of the shelter because the shelter was supposed to be a summerhouse, and you couldn't have people using a summerhouse in winter.

Robin stood by the gates and gaped, with Doggy depending limply from his mouth where he held it by one ear, between his teeth. Anthea decided that if they met anyone she knew, she would explain that Robin was only two, but very big for his age.

"Do you want to run, Robin?"

Robin shook his head.

"There's nothing to be afraid of. You can go all the way round, if you like, but you mustn't walk on the grass or pick things."

Robin nodded. It was the kind of place that he understood.

Anthea sighed. "Well, let's walk round, then."

They set off. At each corner, where the bushes were, the path diverged. One part went in front of the bushes, one part round the back of them. On the first circuit Robin stumped glumly beside Anthea in front of the bushes. The second time round she felt a very faint tug at her hand. Robin wanted to go his own way.

This called for a celebration. Robin could think. Anthea crouched down on the path until they were at the same level.

"You want to walk round the back of the bushes, Robin?"

"Yiss," said Robin.

Robin could *talk*.

"All right, but listen." She lowered her voice to a whisper. "You must be very careful. That path is called Leopard Walk. Do you know what a leopard is?"

"Yiss."

"There are two leopards down there. They live in the bushes. One is a good leopard and the other's a bad leopard. The good leopard has black spots. The bad leopard has red spots. If you see the bad leopard, you must say, 'Die leopard die or I'll kick you in the eye,' and run like anything. Do you understand?"

Robin tugged again.

"Oh no," said Anthea. "I'm going *this* way. If you want to go down Leopard Walk, you'll have to go on your own. I'll meet you at the other end. Remember, if it's got red spots, run like mad."

Robin trotted away. The bushes were just high enough to hide him, but Anthea could see the pompom on his hat doddering along. Suddenly the pompom gathered speed, and Anthea had to run to reach the end of the bushes first.

"Did you see the bad leopard?"

"No," said Robin, but he didn't look too sure.

"Why were you running, then?"

"I just wanted to."

"You've dropped Doggy," said Anthea. Doggy lay on the path with his legs in the air, halfway down Leopard Walk.

"You get him," said Robin.

"No, *you* get him," said Anthea. "I'll wait here." Robin moved off reluctantly. She waited until he had recovered Doggy and then shouted, "I can see the bad leopard in the bushes!" Robin raced back to safety. "Did you say, 'Die leopard die or I'll kick you in the eye'?" Anthea demanded.

"No," Robin said guiltily.

"Then he'll *kill* us," said Anthea. "Come on, run. We've got to get to that tree. He can't hurt us once we're under that tree."

They stopped running under the twisted boughs of a weeping ash. "This is a python tree," said Anthea. "Look, you can see the python wound round the trunk."

"What's a python?" said Robin, backing off.

"Oh, it's just a great big snake that squeezes people to death," said Anthea. "A python could easily eat a leopard. That's why leopards won't walk under this tree, you see, Robin."

Robin looked up. "Could it eat us?"

"Yes, but it won't if we walk on our heels." They walked on their heels to the next corner.

"Are there leopards down there?"

"No, but we must never go down there anyway. That's Poison Alley. All the trees are poisonous. They drip poison. If one bit of poison fell on your head, you'd die."

"I've got my hat on," said Robin, touching the pompom to make sure.

"It would burn right through your hat," Anthea assured him. "Right into your brains. *Fzzzzzzz.*"

They bypassed Poison Alley and walked on over the manhole cover that clanked.

"What's that?"

"That's the Fever Pit. If anyone lifts that manhole cover, they get a terrible disease. There's this terrible disease down there, Robin, and if the lid comes off, the disease will get out and people will die. I should think there's enough disease down there to kill everybody in this town. It's ever so loose, look."

"Don't lift it! Don't lift it!" Robin screamed, and ran to the shelter for safety.

"Don't go in there," yelled Anthea. "That's where the Greasy Witch lives." Robin bounced out of the shelter as though he were on elastic.

"Where's the Greasy Witch?"

"Oh, you can't see her," said Anthea, "but you can tell where she is because she smells so horrible. I think she must be somewhere about. Can't you smell her now?"

Robin sniffed the air and clasped Doggy more tightly.

"And she leaves oily marks wherever she goes. Look, you can see them on the wall."

Robin looked at the wall. Someone had been very busy, if not the Greasy Witch. Anthea was glad on the whole that Robin could not read.

"The smell's getting worse, isn't it, Robin? I think we'd better go down here and then she won't find us."

"She'll see us."

"No, she won't. She can't see with her eyes because they're full of grease. She sees with her ears, but I expect they're all waxy. She's a filthy old witch, really."

They slipped down a secret-looking path that went round the back of the shelter.

"Is the Greasy Witch down here?" said Robin fearfully.

"I don't know," said Anthea. "Let's investigate." They tiptoed round the side of the shelter. The path was damp and slippery. "Filthy old witch. She's certainly *been* here," said Anthea. "I think she's gone now. I'll just have a look."

She craned her neck round the corner of the shelter. There was a sort of glade in the bushes, and in the middle was a standpipe, with a tap on top.

The pipe was wrapped in canvas, like a scaly skin.

"Frightful Corner," said Anthea. Robin put his cautious head round the edge of the shelter.

"What's that?"

Anthea wondered if it could be a dragon, up on the tip of its tail and ready to strike, but on the other side of the bushes was the brick back wall of the King Street Public Conveniences, and at the moment she heard the unmistakable sound of flushing.

"It's a Lavatory Demon," she said. "Quick! We've got to get away before the water stops, or he'll have us."

They ran all the way to the gates, where they could see the church clock, and it was almost time for lunch.

Auntie Lynn fetched Robin home next morning, and three days later she was back again, striding up the path like a warrior queen going into battle, with Robin dangling from her hand and Doggy dangling from Robin's hand.

Mum took her into the front room, closing the door. Anthea sat on the stairs and listened. Auntie Lynn was in full throat and furious, so it was easy enough to hear what she had to say.

"I want a word with that young lady," said Auntie Lynn. "And I want to know what she's been telling him." Her voice dropped, and Anthea could hear only certain fateful words: "Leopards . . . poison trees . . . snakes . . . diseases!"

Mum said something very quietly that Anthea did not hear, and then Auntie Lynn turned up the volume once more.

"Won't go to bed unless I leave the door open... wants the light on... up and down to him all night... won't go to the bathroom on his own. He says the—the—" she hesitated. "The *toilet* demons will get him. He nearly broke his neck running downstairs this morning."

Mum spoke again, but Auntie Lynn cut in like a bandsaw.

"Frightened out of his wits! He follows me everywhere."

The door opened slightly, and Anthea got ready to bolt, but it was Robin who came out, with his thumb in his mouth and circles round his eyes. Under his arm was soggy Doggy, ears chewed to nervous rags.

Robin looked up at Anthea through the banisters.

"Let's go to the park," he said.

Thinking About It

Nothing to Be Afraid Of

1. What is wrong with Robin, and does Anthea's "treatment" make him worse or better?

2. Anthea has the makings of a storyteller. Prove it. If she and Robin do go back to the park, how would you suggest that she change or expand her story?

3. Almost everyone seems to want baby-sitters! Well, what about some unusual ones? Create two advertisements for baby-sitters, one by some children awaiting a baby-sitter, and one by some parents who are going to Europe and want a very responsible baby-sitter.

Another Book by Jan Mark
A family emergency and a trip help give Amy a new view of herself and of her stepfather in *Trouble Half-Way*.

The Invisible Beast
by Jack Prelutsky

The beast that is invisible
is stalking through the park,
but you cannot see it coming
though it isn't very dark.
Oh you know it's out there somewhere
though just why you cannot tell,
but although you cannot see it
it can see you very well.

You sense its frightful features
and its great ungainly form,
and you wish that you were home now
where it's cozy, safe and warm.
And you know it's coming closer
for you smell its awful smell,
and although you cannot see it
it can see you very well.

Oh your heart is beating faster,
beating louder than a drum,
for you hear its footsteps falling
and your body's frozen numb.
And you cannot scream for terror
and your fear you cannot quell,
for although you cannot see it
it can see you very well.

Jabberwocky
by Lewis Carroll

'Twas brillig, and the slithy toves
    Did gyre and gimble in the wabe;
All mimsy were the borogoves,
    And the mome raths outgrabe.

"Beware the Jabberwock, my son!
    The jaws that bite, the claws that catch!
Beware the Jubjub bird, and shun
    The frumious Bandersnatch!"

He took his vorpal sword in hand;
    Long time the manxome foe he sought—
So rested he by the Tumtum tree,
    And stood awhile in thought.

And, as in uffish thought he stood,
    The Jabberwock, with eyes of flame,
Came whiffling through the tulgey wood,
    And burbled as it came!

One, two! One, two! And through and through
    The vorpal blade went snicker-snack!
He left it dead, and with its head
    He went galumphing back.

"And hast thou slain the Jabberwock?
  Come to my arms, my beamish boy!
O frabjous day! Callooh! Callay!"
  He chortled in his joy.

'Twas brillig and the slithy toves
  Did gyre and gimble in the wabe;
All mimsy were the borogoves,
  And the mome raths outgrabe.

THE WISH

by Roald Dahl

Under the palm of one hand the child became aware of the scab of an old cut on his kneecap. He bent forward to examine it closely. A scab was always a fascinating thing; it presented a special challenge he was never able to resist.

Yes, he thought, I will pick it off, even if it isn't ready, even if the middle of it sticks, even if it hurts like anything.

With a fingernail he began to explore cautiously around the edges of the scab. He got the nail underneath it, and when he raised it, but ever so slightly, it suddenly came off, the whole hard brown scab came off beautifully, leaving an interesting little circle of smooth red skin.

Nice. Very nice indeed. He rubbed the circle and it didn't hurt. He picked up the scab, put it on his thigh and flipped it with a finger so that it flew away and landed on the edge of the carpet, the enormous red and black and yellow carpet that stretched the whole length of the hall from the stairs on which he sat to the front door in the distance. A tremendous carpet. Bigger than the tennis lawn. Much bigger than that. He regarded it gravely, settling his eyes upon it with mild pleasure. He had never really noticed it before, but now, all of a sudden, the colors seemed to brighten mysteriously and spring out at him in a most dazzling way.

You see, he told himself, I know how it is. The red parts of the carpet are red-hot lumps of coal. What I must do is this: I must walk all the way along it to the front door without touching them. If I touch the red I will be burnt. As a matter of fact, I will be burnt up completely. And the black parts of the carpet . . . yes, the black parts are snakes, poisonous snakes, adders mostly, and co-bras, thick like tree-trunks round the middle, and if I touch one of *them*, I'll be bitten and I'll die be-fore tea time. And if I get across safely, without being burnt and without being bitten, I will be given a puppy for my birthday tomorrow.

He got to his feet and climbed higher up the stairs to obtain a better view of this vast tapestry of color and death. Was it possible? Was there enough yellow? Yellow was the only color he was allowed to walk on. Could it be done? This was not a journey to be undertaken lightly; the risks were too great for that. The child's face—a fringe of white-gold hair, two large blue eyes, a small pointed chin—peered down anxiously over the banisters. The yellow was a bit thin in places and there were one or two widish gaps, but it did seem to go all the way along to the other end. For someone who had only yesterday trium-phantly travelled the whole length of the brick path from the stables to the summerhouse with-out touching the cracks, this carpet thing should not be too difficult. Except for the snakes. The mere thought of snakes sent a fine electricity of fear running like pins down the backs of his legs and under the soles of his feet.

He came slowly down the stairs and advanced to the edge of the carpet. He extended one small sandalled foot and placed it cautiously upon a patch of yellow. Then he brought the other foot up, and there was just enough room for him to stand with the two feet together. There! He had started! His bright oval face was curiously intent, a shade whiter perhaps than before, and he was holding his arms out sideways to assist his balance. He took another step, lifting his foot high over a patch of black, aiming carefully with his toe for a narrow channel of yellow on the other side. When he had completed the second step he paused to rest, standing very stiff and still. The narrow channel of yellow ran forward unbroken for at least five yards and he advanced gingerly along it, bit by bit, as though walking a tightrope. Where it finally curled off sideways, he had to take another long stride, this time over a vicious-looking mixture of black and red. Halfway across he began to wobble. He waved his arms around wildly, windmill fashion, to keep his balance, and he got across safely and rested again on the other side. He was quite breathless now, and so tense he stood high on his toes all the time, arms out sideways, fists clenched. He was on a big safe island of yellow. There was lots of room on it, he couldn't possibly fall off, and he stood there resting, hesitating, waiting, wishing he could stay forever on this big safe yellow island. But the fear of not getting the puppy compelled him to go on.

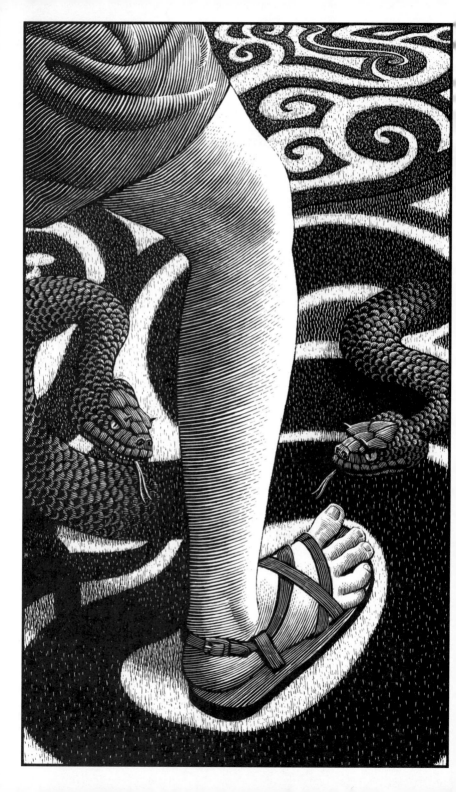

Step by step, he edged further ahead, and between each one he paused to decide exactly where next he should put his foot. Once, he had a choice of ways, either to left or right, and he chose the left because although it seemed the more difficult, there was not so much black in that direction. The black was what made him nervous. He glanced quickly over his shoulder to see how far he had come. Nearly halfway. There could be no turning back now. He was in the middle and he couldn't turn back and he couldn't jump off sideways either because it was too far, and when he looked at all the red and all the black that lay ahead of him, he felt that old sudden sickening surge of panic in his chest—like last Easter time, that afternoon when he got lost all alone in the darkest part of Piper's Wood.

He took another step, placing his foot carefully upon the only little piece of yellow within reach, and this time the point of the foot came within a centimeter of some black. It wasn't touching the black, he could see it wasn't touching, he could see the small line of yellow separating the toe of his sandal from the black; but the snake stirred as though sensing the nearness, and raised its head and gazed at the foot with bright beady eyes, watching to see if it was going to touch.

"I'm not touching you! You mustn't bite me! You know I'm not touching you!"

Another snake slid up noiselessly beside the first, raised its head, two heads now, two pairs of eyes staring at the foot, gazing at a little naked place just below the sandal strap where the skin showed through. The child went high up on his toes and stayed there, frozen stiff with terror. It was minutes before he dared to move again.

The next step would have to be a really long one. There was this deep curling river of black that ran clear across the width of the carpet, and he was forced by this position to cross it at its widest part. He thought first of trying to jump it, but decided he couldn't be sure of landing accurately on the narrow band of yellow the other side. He took a deep breath, lifted one foot, and inch by inch he pushed it out in front of him, far far out, then down and down until at last the tip of his sandal was across and resting safely on the edge of the yellow. He leaned forward, transferring his weight to his front foot. Then he tried to bring the back foot up as well. He strained and pulled and jerked his body, but the legs were too wide apart and he couldn't make it. He tried to get back again. He couldn't do that either. He was doing the splits and he was properly stuck. He glanced down and saw this deep curling river of black underneath him. Parts of it were stirring now, and uncoiling and sliding and beginning to shine with a dreadfully oily glister. He wobbled, waved his arms frantically to keep his balance, but that seemed to make it worse. He was starting to go over. He was going over to the right, quite slowly he was going over, then faster and faster, and at the last moment, instinctively he put out a hand to break the fall and the next thing he saw was this bare hand of his going right into the middle of a great glistening mass of black and he gave one piercing cry of terror as it touched.

Outside in the sunshine, far away behind the house, the mother was looking for her son.

Thinking About It

The Wish

1. As a young child, what games did you make up to amuse yourself? Do you still make up your own games, or do you play games that you buy?

2. How is what the child in "The Wish" does similar to what Anthea does in "Nothing to Be Afraid Of"? Cite evidence from both stories.

3. Create a strange and mysterious pattern for a carpet. What would it be like? What creatures might it suggest?

AMERICAN WEATHER

Interviews by Charles Kuralt

Well, the sun was shining a few minutes ago, but now it looks like there's a big storm coming. Mark Twain, remarking on American weather, said one time that he sat in one place and counted 136 different kinds of weather inside of twenty-four hours. That may be an exaggeration. When it comes to the weather, Americans do tend to exaggerate. So, when we decided to do a national weather survey, we sought out only exceptionally truthful individuals like my friend Roger Welsch, a Nebraska tree farmer and keen observer of Nebraska weather.

KURALT: When the real dog days come, it does get hot in Nebraska.

ROGER WELSCH: I don't think there's any place hotter than Nebraska in the summer. Down here by the river, just not too far from us, it'll get so dry that the catfish will come up here to the house and get a drink at the pump. Yep, really. Yeah. And a lot of the farmers around here will feed their chickens cracked ice so they won't lay hard-boiled eggs.

Well you may laugh, but the hot weather leads to tragedy sometimes. Kendall Morse remembers what happened in Maine.

KENDALL MORSE: Oh, it was so hot here in Maine last summer that one day—it was right in the middle of corn season, that corn was almost ripe—and it got so hot that the corn started to pop, and it popped and it went all over the place. And there was a herd of cows right next to that cornfield and they looked up and they saw that popcorn coming down like that. And cows are not very bright, of course. They thought it was snow. And every one of them idiot cows stood there and froze to death!

For Maine, of course, that was a hot day. Here's a Hoosier weather report from Charles Porter.

CHARLES PORTER: It was so hot here one day in Odon, Indiana, you could take a frozen hamburger patty out of the freezer, toss it up in the air, and when it came down it was cooked well done. But you had to be careful and not toss it up too high. If you did, it came back down burned. *[Chuckles]*

We went to Arizona in midsummer to ask Jim Griffith how he and his neighbors are holding up.

JIM GRIFFITH: It does get a little bit warm. Joe Harris says it usually gets so hot and dry in the summertime that he's got to prime himself before he can spit. And the dog's sort of wandering around at midnight trying to find some shade to lay down in. It does warm up a little bit, but you get used to it. It's been known, especially in this part of Arizona, to get so dry that the trees will follow the dogs around.

That's dry, all right. But right there in Nebraska, Roger Welsch's wife has to run their well through

a wringer this time of year to get enough water to cook with. And the river gets low, of course.

WELSCH: They talk about frogs that would grow up to be three and four years old without ever having learned how to swim. And they'd have to, in the schools, you know, get little cans and put holes in the bottom and sprinkle water so that kids could see what it was and wouldn't panic the first time they saw it rain. They tell about one farmer who's out plowing one day and it started to rain, and the first drops that hit him shocked him so that he passed out. And to bring him to, they had to throw two buckets of dust in his face!

Oh, it's been a dry summer, but it sure was a wet spring. Don Reed remembers how wet it got in the Middle West.

DON REED: In Minnesota, the floods were so bad that the turtles crawled out of their shells and used the shells as rowboats.

PORTER: The raindrops were so big here one day, it only took one raindrop to fill a quart jar. *[Laughs]*

Big as those Indiana raindrops were, they weren't as big as some Ed Bell remembers from a Texas storm back in '73.

ED BELL: There was one place there that I noticed raindrops nearly as big as a number-three wash-tub and they formed a kind of a marching pattern coming straight down, one right behind the other, and it wore a hole in the ground that we used for a well. And ten years later, we are still drawing rainwater out of that well.

What rain they get in the Great Plains comes all at once, eight or ten inches in one day and that's it for the year. Every farmer has a little lane out to the highway and the rains on the plains fall mainly on the lanes.

WELSCH: Like this road of mine, there's some holes out here you can run set lines in and catch fish out of the road. And there's one farmer who talked about finally having to walk into town, because his wagon wouldn't get up his lane. So, he had to walk into town to get some groceries, and he found this huge puddle out in the middle of his road. And there was a nice hat floating around in the center. So, he reached out with his foot and kicked in this hat, and there was a guy's head under it. So, he got down on his hands and knees and he said, "Are you all right, stranger?" And the guy said, "Well, I guess so. I'm on horseback." [Laughs]

Wherever you got puddles like that, of course, you get mosquitos. I thought we had big mosquitos back home in North Carolina. My grandfather told me he saw a couple once the size of crows, and heard 'em talking about him. One of those mosquitos said, "Shall we eat him here or take him with us?" The other one said, "Well, we better eat him here. If we take him with us, the big guys will take him away from us." What surprised me was to learn that they grow mosquitos bigger than that out West.

JIM GRIFFITH: They get reasonably good-sized, not so big that you can't shoot 'em down with a scatter gun. You know, you don't have to take a rifle to 'em, but they get pretty good-sized. But the

really big ones are up in southern Nevada. There was one, I remember, it was in the papers at the time, there was one that come in to Nellis Air Force Base up there, and they filled it up with high-octane fuel before they realized that it had the wrong markings on it. And—

KURALT [laughing]: That was a big mosquito.

GRIFFITH: That was a good-sized mosquito, yeah. That was pretty good-sized.

I should mention again I'm not sure all these stories are true. Americans do lie sometimes. There was a fellow down home with such a reputation for lying that he had to have a neighbor come in to call his hogs. But if these aren't true stories, they're about as true as any other weather reports you're likely to hear.

In the middle of August, it's easy to forget how cold it was last winter. A friend of mine who lives in a cabin in Montana told me it was so cold there that the flame froze on his candle and he had to take it outside and bury it to get it dark enough to sleep. Sidney Boyum says it was cold in Wisconsin, too.

SIDNEY BOYUM: It was so cold here in Madison that a night crawler came out of the ground, mugged the caterpillar, stole his fur coat, and went back into the ground.

You know it's cold when you see something like that happen. In Maine, Joe Perham says it was an awful quiet winter.

JOE PERHAM: Well, it was so cold last winter up here in Maine that the words froze right in our mouths. That's right. We had to wait till spring to find out what we'd been talking about all winter.

The real old-timers remember a winter like that in Nebraska. They still talk about the blizzard of '88.

WELSH: The worst part was the first day of spring, 'cause you couldn't hear yourself think, for all the rooster crows and train whistles that were thawing out. Another guy said, no, the worst part was milking, because he said it was so cold that when you milked, the milk would freeze before it hit the bottom of the bucket; and another guy said, well, they learned how to deal with that in their family. They'd milk with one arm out. They'd milk out over their arm until they had an armload of frozen squirts. And they'd tie that up with binder twine and put it up in the barn till their mother was cooking and she'd send them out for however many squirts the recipe called for. [Laughs]

Arizonans are not much troubled by cold weather, of course. But that desert is about the *windiest* place I've ever been.

KURALT [as gusts blow the sand]: Does the wind always blow this way?
GRIFFITH: Well, no, Charles. About half the time it backs around and blows the other way. In the summertime, the west wind blows so darn hard that it causes the sun to set three hours later than it does in the wintertime.
KURALT [to Welsch]: I guess the wind blows here in Nebraska sometimes, huh?

WELSCH: All the time. They say one day the wind stopped and everybody fell down.

Ed Bell says they had a pretty good windstorm in Texas just this spring.

BELL: Folks, that was a wind! That wind blew and blew and blew. It just got harder and harder; blew the bark off the trees, blew all the feathers off of chickens, even blew the four tires off the old Model-T Ford; turned a bulldog wrong side out.

REED: A fellow in northern Wisconsin wrote that in 1976 they had a windstorm so bad that it stretched his telephone wires so far that when he called his neighbor across the street, he was billed $17.60 plus tax for long distance telephone charges.

PORTER: I was out in the front yard one day and we had a windstorm came through there. That wind was so strong, it blew a big iron kettle across the front yard so fast, the lightning had to strike it five times before it got a hit. [Laughs]

WELSCH: Easterners often notice that in Nebraska, unlike other parts of the country, there aren't wind vanes on the barns, 'cause what you normally do is look out and see which way the barn is leaning, and that will tell you which way the wind's blowing. But they do have a Nebraska wind directional teller, which is a post in the ground with a logging chain on the end, and then you just watch to see which way the logging chain blows to tell which way the wind's from. And you can tell the wind speed by how many links are being snapped off at the end. [Laughs]

Well, of course, you'd expect the wind to blow hard in Nebraska, because there's nothing between there and the North Pole but a couple of barbed wire fences. And if somebody leaves one of the gates open, then there's nothing to stop the wind, all the way down.

PERHAM: Wind? Well, the wind blew so hard here last night that the hen laid the same egg four times.

Laid the same egg four times. That was in Maine. This is Chuck Larkin, who lives in Georgia.

CHUCK LARKIN: I seen a chicken, just this afternoon, standing with her back to the wind, laid the same egg five times.

Five times in Georgia!

WELSCH: The other day someone told me that they had a chicken here that laid the same egg seven times.

Seven times in Nebraska!

GRIFFITH: Old Joe was raising chickens and first thing that happened was that he got 'em back the wrong way in the wind, and the old hen laid the same egg fourteen times over before she finally got it out.

Fourteen times in Arizona! I told you Arizona was the windiest place of all! But then, it's a pretty windy country, as you may have noticed.

Thinking About It

American Weather

1. Have you heard anyone exaggerate about the weather? Have you done such a thing? Do you have anything to add to Charles Kuralt's account? What "ran through your mind" as you read this article?

2. Suppose you transport Charles Kuralt's article into another medium. What would the medium be, and how would you make the interviews interesting?

3. You can become a part of folklore! All you need to do is to tell or write a lively description of some high point in the weather where you live. Do it now. Become a part of folklore history.

Fish Story
by Richard Armour

Count this among my heartfelt wishes:
To hear a fish tale told by fishes
And stand among the fish who doubt
The honor of a fellow trout.

And watch the bulging of their eyes
To hear of imitation flies
And worms with rather droopy looks
Stuck through with hateful, horrid hooks.
And fishermen they fled all day from
(As big as this) and got away from.

Excursion
by Eve Merriam

A dancing bear at a summer fair
conversed with a jumping flea.

"It's hot and, ugh, the humidity,
*   my fur gets matted," complained the bear.*

"I sorely agree, for I itch,"
*   said the flea.*
"Shall we travel together
*   to cooler weather?*
*   A breeze from the Arctic*
*   might well be cathartic."*

"Let's take it on the lam,"
*   declared the bear.*
"Split, vamoose,
*   scat and skedaddle.*
*   With no more ado,*
*   let's be begone*
*   to Seattle and Saskatchewan.*
*   We could go as far north*
*   as the Firth of Forth."*

Said the flea with glee,
"We'll be refreshed and we can say
*   we wish each other an ice day."*

The Story of
Arachne and Minerva

THE WEAVING CONTEST

Myth retold by
Mary Pope Osborne

Arachne, a proud peasant girl, was a wonderful spinner and weaver of wool. The water nymphs journeyed from their rivers and the wood nymphs from their forests just to watch Arachne steep her wool in crimson dyes, then take the long threads in her skillful fingers and weave exquisite tapestries.

"Ah! Minerva must have given you your gift!" declared a wood nymph one day. Minerva was the goddess of weaving and handicrafts.

Arachne threw back her head. "Ha! Minerva has taught me nothing! I've taught myself everything I know!" And with that, she decided to challenge Minerva to a contest. "Let's see which of us should be called 'goddess of the loom'!" she said.

The nymphs covered their mouths, frightened to hear such scorn heaped upon a powerful goddess of Mount Olympus.

Their fears were justified—for Minerva herself was furious when word got back to her about Arachne's conceit. The goddess immediately donned the disguise of an old woman with gray hair and hobbled with a cane to Arachne's cottage.

When Arachne opened her door, Minerva shook her gnarled finger. "If I were you," said the old woman, "I would not compare myself so favorably to the great goddess Minerva. I would feel humble toward her and ask her to pardon my prideful arrogance."

"You silly fool!" said Arachne. "What do you mean by coming to my door and telling me what to do? If that goddess is half so great as the world thinks, let her come here and show me!"

"She is here!" boomed a powerful voice, and before Arachne's eyes, the old woman instantly changed into the goddess Minerva.

Arachne's face flushed with shame. Nevertheless she remained defiant and plunged headlong toward her doom. "Hello, Minerva," she said. "Do you dare to finally weave against me?"

Minerva only glared at the girl, as the nymphs, peeking from behind the trees, cringed to watch such insolence.

"Come in if you like," Arachne said, stepping back from her doorway and bidding the goddess to enter. Without speaking, Minerva went into

the cottage. Servants quickly dashed about, setting up two looms. Then Arachne and Minerva tucked up their long dresses and set to work. Their busy fingers flew back and forth as they each wove rainbows of colors: dark purples, pinks, golds, and crimsons.

Minerva wove a tapestry showing the twelve greatest gods and goddesses of Mount Olympus. But Arachne wove a tapestry showing not only the gods and goddesses, but their adventures also. Then she bordered her magnificent work with flowers and ivy.

The river nymphs and wood nymphs stared in awe at Arachne's tapestry. Her work was clearly better than Minerva's. Even the goddess Envy, who haughtily inspected it, said, "There is no flaw."

When she heard Envy's words, Minerva lost her temper. The goddess tore Arachne's tapestry and hit her mercilessly—until disgraced and humiliated, Arachne crawled away and tried to hang herself.

At last, moved to a little pity, Minerva said, "You may live, Arachne, but you will hang forever—and do your weaving in the air!"

Then the vengeful goddess sprinkled Arachne with hellbane; and the girl's hair fell off, and her nose and ears fell off. Her head shrank to a tiny size until she was mostly a giant belly. But her fingers could still weave; and within minutes, Arachne, the first spider on earth, wove the first magnificent web.

Thinking About It

The Weaving Contest

1. Clever characters are to be found in clever stories. Describe a character who might be clever enough to match wits with Arachne.

2. Stories are told through conversation and sound-and-visual effects. Think of some other way to communicate this story. What special effects would you use to enhance the story?

3. Imagine a modern setting for "The Weaving Contest." What would it be like? In what ways would the characters have to change? What might their new roles or occupations be?

*Legend from the Miskito Indians
of Nicaragua*

THE INVISIBLE HUNTERS

As told by Harriet Rohmer

Late one Saturday afternoon, three brothers left the village of Ulwas on the Coco River in Nicaragua. They were going to hunt wari, the wild pig which is so delicious to eat.

After walking an hour through the bush, they heard a voice.

"Dar. Dar. Dar," said the voice.

The brothers stopped. They looked around, but there was nobody there. Then they heard the voice again.

"Dar. Dar. Dar."

The voice came from a vine that was swinging from a tree in front of them.

The first brother grabbed the vine. Instantly, he disappeared. Then the second brother grabbed the vine and he disappeared.

The third brother cried out in fear, "What have you done with my brothers?"

"I have not harmed your brothers," answered the voice. "When they let go of me, you will see them."

The first two brothers let go of the vine. Instantly they became visible again.

"Who are you?" demanded the brothers in amazement.

"I am the Dar," said the voice. "When you hold me, neither human nor animal can see you."

The brothers quickly understood how the Dar could help them.

"We could sneak up on the wari and they wouldn't see us."

"Then we could kill them easily with our sticks."

Each of the brothers wanted a piece of the Dar. They grabbed for it, but the vine swung away from them and disappeared.

"Before you take my power, you must promise to use it well," said the Dar.

"We will promise anything," said the brothers.

"First, you must promise never to sell the wari meat. You must give it away. Then, you must promise never to hunt with guns. You must hunt only with sticks."

The brothers had never sold wari meat. They had always given it to the people. They had never hunted with guns. They had always hunted with sticks. They knew no other way.

"We promise," they said. So the Dar allowed each one of them to take away a small piece of the magic vine.

That day, the brothers had great success in the hunt. After killing many wari, they hung their pieces of the Dar on the tree and started for home.

The people of Ulwas welcomed the brothers with much rejoicing. They cleaned the animals and hung them above the fire. Soon, the delicious smell of smoking meat reached every house in the village. When the meat was ready, the brothers cut it in pieces and shared it with everyone. Never had the people of Ulwas eaten so well.

Later that night, the elders of the village asked the brothers how they had killed so many wari. The brothers told them about their promises to the Dar.

"This is truly good fortune," said the elders. "We have heard of this vine. It is very old and powerful. As long as you keep your promises, our village will prosper and our people will honor you."

With the help of the Dar, the brothers became famous hunters. Stories about them spread to all the villages along the Coco River and even beyond.

One day, a boat carrying two strangers arrived at Ulwas. The strangers greeted the brothers and gave them presents—bright-colored cloth and barrels of wine.

"We have traveled many days to meet such great hunters," they said.

The brothers invited the men to eat with them. After they had eaten, the strangers told the brothers that they were traders. They had come to buy wari meat.

"We cannot sell the wari," said the brothers, remembering their promise to the Dar. "That is what our people eat."

The traders laughed. "We never expected that such great hunters would be so foolish. Of course your people have to eat. We only want to buy what they don't eat."

The brothers were tempted. "Maybe we could

sell just a little meat," said the first brother.

"But the Dar will know," said the second brother.

The brothers looked at each other nervously. Then the third brother said, "We have seen that the traders are clever men. Their power must be greater than the power of the Dar."

The brothers nodded. It would not be wise to displease the traders.

So the brothers began to sell the wari.

The traders returned many times to the village of Ulwas. Each time they brought more money for the hunters. Each time they took away more wari. Soon the brothers were worried that there was not enough wari for the people.

The traders laughed at their worries. "It is your own fault for hunting with sticks," they said.

"But we have always hunted with sticks."

"That is why you cannot feed your people. You need to kill the wari faster. You need guns."

The brothers talked things over. "If we bought guns, we could kill more wari," said the first brother. "We could sell to the traders and feed the people too."

"But what will happen to us?" asked the second brother.

The third brother laughed before he answered. "We will become clever men—like the traders."

So the brothers began to hunt with guns. They had completely forgotten their promise to the Dar.

Little by little their hearts turned away from the people. The more meat they brought home, the more they sold to the traders. They were becoming accustomed to the things that money could buy.

The elders of the village spoke sternly to the brothers. "You must feed the people. They are hungry."

The brothers answered angrily, "If they want meat, they can pay us for it like the traders do!"

But the people had no money. They began to wait for the hunters outside the village. When the hunters returned loaded down with wari, the people demanded meat.

"Clever men do not give away what they can sell," said the hunters to each other. So they gave the people spoiled meat, which they could not sell.

The people were angry. "Are you no longer our brothers?" they shouted.

The hunters laughed and went on their way. They even pushed aside the elders who tried to reason with them.

Many months passed. One day when the brothers returned to the village, the people did not crowd around them as usual. Instead they backed away. Some covered their eyes and screamed. Others stared in disbelief at the strange procession of dead wari moving slowly through the air. Only the elders understood what had happened.

"The Dar has made the hunters invisible," they said.

It was true. The brothers were invisible. They had left their pieces of Dar at the tree as they always did, but they were still invisible. Something had gone wrong.

They dropped the animals they were carrying and raced through the bush to the tree.

"What have you done?" they asked the Dar in terror.

But the Dar did not answer them.

The brothers fell to their knees and begged for help.

But the Dar only repeated its name over and over.

"Dar. Dar. Dar."

Then the brothers realized what terrible things they had done, and they were ashamed. Tearfully, they made their way home.

Outside the village the elders were waiting. The brothers pleaded for forgiveness, but the elders did not forgive them.

"From this moment on, you are banished from Ulwas," they said. "Never again will you live with us."

The brothers begged the elders for one more chance. "How can we live away from our people?" they cried.

But the elders turned their backs on them and walked away.

So the invisible hunters left their village forever. They wandered up the Coco River as far as the falls at Carizal. As they wandered, they called out to the Dar, begging to become visible again.

Some of the Miskito people from the Coco River say that the hunters are still wandering after all these years. A few even say that the invisible hunters have passed them in the bush. They know it is true, they say, because they have heard voices calling, "Dar. Dar. Dar."

About the Story

Harriet Rohmer

Harriet Rohmer

The legend of *The Invisible Hunters* documents the first moments of contact between the native culture of the region and the outside world. While this story takes place in the Miskito Indian village of Ulwas in northern Nicaragua, it is also a metaphor —or implied comparison —for what has happened to traditional cultures in many other parts of the world.

The story came to me in fragments. My research turned up references to a wandering band of invisible Miskito hunters. I asked about them on my first visit to the Atlantic Coast of Nicaragua in 1983, but without success. Fortunately, my quest came to the attention of Father Agustin Sambola, an Afro-Indian Catholic priest who was greatly respected by the Miskitos in the north. He invited me to accompany him on a visit to the outlying Miskito communities of his parish.

As I was about to join Agustin in January, 1984, word came that his jeep had been ambushed by "contra" mercenaries who were trying to overthrow the Nicaraguan government. Miraculously, he was unhurt. The journey went off as planned. In the mining town of La Rosita, I met Octavio Chow, an elder Miskito Catholic deacon who knew of the story and added to it. Speaking in Miskito, which his son Martin translated into Spanish, Octavio told me about the magic Dar vine that gives whoever holds it the power of invisibility.

Was there someone who could tell me more of the story? On my return to the capital city of Managua, Bishop John Wilson of the Protestant Moravian Church, himself part Miskito, arranged for a meeting with a lay pastor who had grown up in a Miskito village on the Atlantic Coast and was a leader in his community. "According to the stories I heard as a child," he told me, "the Dar has a voice. I can take you to people who say they have heard that voice."

Several years have passed since I began to put together this tale. I hope it will fascinate you as it has fascinated me. More than that, I hope that the young North Americans who read this story will gain a new understanding and respect for the people of Central America. For without understanding and respect there can be no hope for peace with dignity in our hemisphere.

Thinking About It

The Invisible Hunters

1. Have you ever wished to be invisible? Why might you or others want to be invisible, and for how long and where?

2. People can't really become invisible as the hunters do, yet the message in this story had real-life meaning for the people who told it in the Miskito Indian village of Nicaragua. Explain why.

3. "The Invisible Hunters" has meaning for people today as it did for the Miskito Indians who first told the story. Suppose the setting is North America and the time is now. What occupations might the hunters have? What changes would you make in the story?

ABOUT EARTH HAPPENINGS

by Gretchen Will Mayo

Earth events have astonished, puzzled, terrified, and tormented people since the world began.

Tornadoes roared into the camps of our ancestors. Earthquakes rattled their bones. Storm clouds threatened destruction, and rainbows signaled calm.

From the beginning, the wise ones searched for ways to explain these things. "Why did Earthmaker bring the storm?" the Winnebago asked; and, "Who has made Earthmaker angry?" Their reasoning led to stories that helped to make sense of puzzling and frightening events.

Stories also made people laugh and forget their worries. Indians, often wonderfully creative, shared and traded their tales from tribe to tribe or with people who were not Native Americans. Because early Indians had not developed a written language, it was the European missionaries and explorers who usually recorded their stories for the first time. The tales, however, were not always written exactly as they were told. On the other hand, loving a good story, Indians wove parts of some European folktales into their own. Some legends, of course, were sacred and could never be given away or changed, even to this day.

In early days, the time and setting for storytelling was very important. Rules had to be followed, although the rules varied from tribe to tribe.

Like many other tribes, the Blackfoot insisted on telling their legends after dark and in the winter time. Stories often continued far into the night, lengthened and embellished with details and colorful descriptions. The Yavapai of central Arizona considered it dangerous to tell their stories during the summer months, when spiders and snakes might hear and bite them. They waited for storytelling until autumn, when the animals began their long sleep and couldn't listen. Then they built a good fire and sat in a circle around one of the elders of the tribe, a keeper of the old stories.

*Folk Tale from the Apache People
Told by Laforia*

BIG ELK DIGS UP THE MOUNTAINS

As retold by Gretchen Will Mayo

There are many Native American tales explaining how the mountains came to be. In some, when the soft earth was being formed, Coyote ran all over leaving his footprints and digging up the mud. In those tribes living near volcanoes, the mountains were often said to be living, growing beings who became angry and even ate people.

The Apache lived in the dry plains area just east of the high mountains. In their stories, the first people came up from the underworld and found the earth inhabited by monsters. Like most tribes, the Apache believed the sun was a being with immense power. Sun's son also had special powers, but he was more like the people and was often called to help them.

In the earliest times, all the land on earth was flat, and all the animals were gigantic monsters. Big Elk was the most terrible of all. He sprawled across the warm dry plain and gobbled up people for snacks.

The people cried out to the gods for help, so Father Sun sent his own son to see what he could do. Son of Sun crept to Big Elk's resting place to watch from behind some tall dry grass. There were no bushes or trees on the open plain, and Son of Sun wondered how he could creep closer without being seen. As he sat and pondered, Lizard, who was sunning on a rock nearby, called out, "What are you doing here, my friend?"

"My father sent me to help the people," explained the surprised son of the sun. He told Lizard how Big Elk had been gobbling the people one-by-one. "But the plain is so flat and bare," he said. "How can I get close enough to shoot Big Elk with my arrows?"

Lizard's beady eyes blinked. "The desert is home to us lizards. We sun on the rocks and rest in the shade. There are so many of us, Elk hardly notices."

"But why doesn't he gobble you like he gobbles the people?" asked Son of Sun.

"Why do I eat flies?" answered Lizard, with a flick of his long tongue. "It's just a question of taste. Maybe if you looked like a lizard, Big Elk wouldn't want you for a snack either," suggested Lizard. He wriggled out of his coat and offered it to Son of Sun.

The son of the sun squeezed one arm into Lizard's tight coat. As he was tugging at the other, the ground beneath him heaved, and up popped Gopher, knocking Son of Sun right off his feet!

"Why were you standing right over the door to my tunnel?" huffed Gopher.

"Why did you dig your door right under my feet?" answered Son of Sun.

Then Gopher peered hard at Son of Sun. "Why on earth are you wearing Lizard's coat?" she sniffed.

The son of the sun explained why he had come to the desert plain. "If Big Elk makes a meal of me, I won't be much help to the people," he said, "so Lizard gave me his coat."

"My, my, my," sighed Gopher. "To Elk you'll just look like a tasty snack in a coat that doesn't fit. But maybe I can help. If you follow my tunnel, Big Elk will never see you."

With this, Gopher dove back into her hole. Dirt flew and the ground quivered, but soon Son of Sun could see the path of a long tunnel winding across the flat plain toward the giant elk.

Gopher was gone a long time.

Even when the burrow reached the place where Big Elk rested, Gopher did not return.

"Maybe Big Elk gobbles gophers too," thought Son of Sun mournfully. Then suddenly the ground heaved again and up popped Gopher, knocking Son of Sun right off his feet.

"Why do you always stand over my door?" huffed Gopher.

"Why do you always dig your door right under my feet?" answered Son of Sun.

Then Gopher peered hard at the son of the sun. "Stop asking so many questions," she sniffed. "Go after Big Elk!"

So the son of the sun plunged into Gopher's tunnel, following it far under the dry, flat plain.

Thumpa, thumpa, THUMPA, THUMPA!

A terrible pounding overhead shook the earth around him. Son of Sun looked up and saw Elk's hide thumping right over his head. This was the beating of Big Elk's giant heart! Gopher had brought him to a spot right under the monster elk.

Without wasting a moment, the son of the sun drew his bow. Four times his arrows shot above.

But to giant Big Elk, they were like the sting of four bees. The angry elk rose up on his four tall legs to see who was stinging him and he looked right down into Gopher's tunnel at the son of the sun!

"Oh, no!" yelled Son of Sun as the enraged giant plunged his giant antler into Gopher's tunnel. The son of the sun turned in the tunnel and ran for his life.

Furious, Big Elk gouged his way along the burrowed path after Son of Sun, ploughing up mountains of dry brown earth with his sharp antlers.

Son of Sun ran and ran. When he came to the end of the tunnel, Big Elk was right behind him. But Big Black Spider was able to help the son of the sun. He lowered a tight, strong web and blocked the charging elk so that Son of Sun could get away.

By now the monster elk was so angry that he went right on ploughing up the earth, gashing and rutting from one end of the land to the other until finally he gasped his last raging breath and dropped dead.

Son of Sun thanked Big Black Spider and the people thanked Son of Sun. From that time on, the children of fearsome Big Elk were much smaller. Father Sun ruled that his elk children would eat grasses and plants rather than people. But some things remained the same. Gopher still digs tunnels. Lizard still suns on the desert rocks. And the tall mountains ploughed by Big Elk still stand high above the flat, dry plains.

Thinking About It

About Earth Happenings
Big Elk Digs Up the Mountains

1. Early Native Americans told tales to explain things in nature they didn't understand. What things in the world cause you to wonder?

2. In what ways are the selections you've read so far in this book alike? Why do you think "American Weather" is included?

3. Create a story that explains how something in nature came to be. Consider things such as rivers, rain, or wind. What part would Son of Sun play? What animals might be in the story?

A Book of Tales
If you enjoyed this tale, you may want to read other North American Indian stories in *Earthmaker's Tales* by Gretchen Will Mayo.

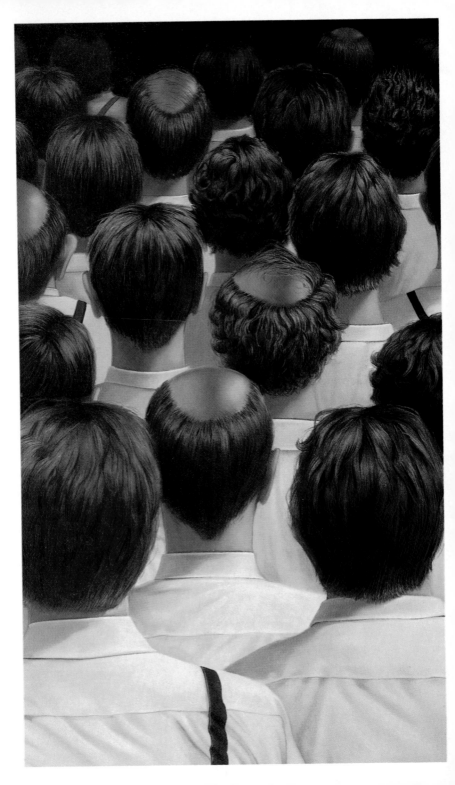

SHERLOCK HOLMES
AND THE
RED-HEADED LEAGUE

Play by Lewy Olfson
Based on the story by Arthur Conan Doyle

Characters

NARRATOR
SHERLOCK HOLMES
DR. WATSON
JABEZ WILSON
VINCENT SPAULDING
DUNCAN ROSS
LANDLORD

NARRATOR: Dr. Watson, opening the door of Sherlock Holmes's Baker Street rooms, finds Holmes seated beside a man with the reddest hair he has ever seen. . . .

HOLMES: Ah, Watson, you could not have come at a better time. Here is a gentleman I should like you to meet. Mr. Wilson, this is Dr. Watson, my partner and helper in many of my most successful cases, and I have no doubt that he will be of the utmost use to me in yours also. Watson, this is Mr. Jabez Wilson.

WATSON: How do you do, Mr. Wilson?

WILSON: I'm so glad to meet you, Dr. Watson.

HOLMES: Try the settee, Watson. You know, since in the past you have shown such extraordinary interest in everything that is outside the conventions and humdrum routine of everyday life, I'm sure you will particularly enjoy the details of this case.

WATSON: Ah, Holmes, you know your cases have been of the greatest interest to me. But what is this particular case about?

HOLMES: Mr. Wilson here has been good enough to call upon me this morning, and to begin a narrative which promises to be one of the most singular which I have listened to for some time. Perhaps, Mr. Wilson, you would be kind enough to begin your tale again because my friend, Dr. Watson, has not heard the beginning of the tale.

WILSON: I shall be happy to do so, Mr. Holmes.

HOLMES: Can you find the advertisement you spoke of in that newspaper again?

WILSON: Yes, I have it now. Here it is. This is what began it all, Dr. Watson. Here. Just read it for yourself.

WATSON (Reading aloud): "To the Red-Headed League. On account of the bequest of the late Ezekiah Hopkins, of Lebanon, Pennsylvania, U.S.A., there is now another vacancy open which entitles a member of the League to a salary of four pounds a week for purely nominal services. All red-headed men who are sound in body and mind, and above the age of twenty-one, are eligible. Apply in person on Monday, at eleven o'clock, to Duncan Ross, at the offices of the League, 7 Pope's Court, Fleet Street."

HOLMES: Curious, is it not?

WATSON: Well, what does it mean?

HOLMES: That is what we must find out. But before I ask Mr. Wilson to relate any more, I ask you, Watson, to note the paper and the date.

WATSON: It is the *Morning Chronicle* of April 27, 1890. Just two months ago.

HOLMES: Very good. Now, Mr. Wilson?

WILSON: It is just as I have been telling Mr. Sherlock Holmes. I have a small pawnbroker's business at Coburg Square. Of late years it has not done more than give me a bare living.

HOLMES: Do you work in it alone?

WILSON: No, I have an assistant—though, to tell the truth, I should not be able to employ him if he did not agree to work for such low pay.

HOLMES: What is his name?

WILSON: His name is Vincent Spaulding, and I should not wish a smarter assistant. He could earn better money elsewhere—but, if he's satisfied, I'm not the one to put ideas in his head. He has his faults, too. Never was such a fellow for photography. Snapping away with his camera, and then diving down into the cellar to develop his pictures. That is his main fault, but on the whole he's a good worker.

WATSON: He is still with you, I presume, sir?

WILSON: Yes, he is. We live very quietly, the two of us—for I'm widowed, with no family—and we keep a roof over our heads and pay our debts if we do nothing more. The first thing that interrupted our dull and quiet lives was this advertisement. As a matter of fact, it was my assistant, Vincent Spaulding, himself, who called it to my attention.

HOLMES: How was that?

WILSON: Vincent Spaulding came into the office just this day eight weeks ago with this very paper in his hand, and he said . . .

SPAULDING (*A young, vigorous voice*): Mr. Wilson, I wish that I were a red-headed man.

WILSON: Why should you wish that, Vincent?

SPAULDING: Why, here's another vacancy in the Red-Headed League. It's worth quite a little fortune to any man who qualifies, and I understand they can never find enough men with hair of just the right shade. Why, if my hair would only change to the same color that your hair is, I could step into a nice fortune.

WILSON: I've never heard of it. What is it then?

SPAULDING: I wonder that *you* don't know of it, for you're eligible yourself for one of the vacancies, what with your flaming red hair.

WILSON: What are the vacancies worth?

SPAULDING: Merely a couple of hundred pounds a year—but the work is slight, and wouldn't interfere with other occupations.

WILSON: Tell me about it. A couple of hundred a year would certainly come in handy.

SPAULDING: As far as I can make out, the League was founded by an American millionaire who was very peculiar in his ways. He was himself of red hair, and wanted to make life easier for those who were like him. From all that I hear, it is splendid pay and very little to do.

WILSON: There would be millions of red-haired men that would apply.

SPAULDING: Not so many as you might think. You see, it is confined to grown men, from London, which was the American's native city. And as for color, why, the man's hair must be bright, blazing, fiery red like yours . . .

WILSON: "Bright, blazing, fiery red like yours." Yes, Mr. Holmes and Dr. Watson, those were the very words he used. You can readily see for yourselves that my hair is of a full, rich color, so I decided, upon Spaulding's urging, that I would have a try at it.

HOLMES: What happened after that, Mr. Wilson?

WILSON: Well, sir, I went to the specified address at the appointed time, accompanied by my assistant, Spaulding. Let me say that I never hope to see a sight such as that again. From all corners of London had come every man who had a shade of red in his hair. I didn't think there were so many in the whole country as were brought together by that advertisement. Every shade of color, they were—straw, lemon, orange, brick, Irish-setter, liver, clay—but, as Spaulding pointed out, none was as bright as my own. Well, sir, we pushed and pulled and jammed our way forward, and finally found ourselves next in line at the office door.

HOLMES: Your experience has been a most entertaining one, Wilson.

WATSON: Indeed, yes! Pray continue your story!

WILSON: The office itself was a small one—nothing particular about it. Behind the desk sat a man whose hair was redder than mine—a Mr. Duncan Ross, he told me later. As we entered the office, he shut the door, and said . . .

ROSS: Your name, sir?

WILSON: Mr. Jabez Wilson, and willing to fill a vacancy in the League.

ROSS: You are admirably suited for it, Mr. Wilson. I cannot recall when I have seen a red head so fine. May I take hold of your hair, sir?

WILSON: Certainly, if you like.

ROSS (As if pulling): Ugh! Mph! No, it's yours all right. I am sorry to have had to take this precaution, but we have twice been deceived by wigs, and once by dye.

WILSON: Oh, no, sir. My hair is my own.

SPAULDING: Indeed it is, sir.

ROSS: Well, then, Mr. Wilson. My name is Duncan Ross, and I am myself one of the pensioners upon the fund left by our noble benefactor. I am pleased to tell you that the position is yours. When shall you be able to enter upon your new duties?

WILSON: It is a little awkward, for I have a business already.

SPAULDING: Never mind that, Mr. Wilson. I shall look after that for you.

WILSON: What would the hours be, Mr. Ross?

ROSS: From ten to two.

WILSON: A pawnbroker's business—for that is my trade—is done mostly at night. So I suppose I can trust my shop to my assistant here. Yes, yes, Spaulding, you're a good man. Yes, ten to two would suit me very well. And the pay?

ROSS: Four pounds a week.

WILSON: And the work?

ROSS: The work is to copy out the *Encyclopaedia Britannica*. Don't ask me why: it is the terms of the will. You must provide your own pens, paper and ink, but we provide the table and chair. Also, you forfeit the position if you once leave

the building during the hours of ten to two. Will you be ready tomorrow?

WILSON: Certainly.

ROSS: Then goodbye, Mr. Jabez Wilson, and let me congratulate you once more on the important position which you have been fortunate enough to obtain. And welcome to the Red-Headed League . . .

WILSON: With those words, gentlemen, he bowed me and my assistant out of the room. I was, at the same time, both pleased and puzzled.

WATSON: Pleased and puzzled? How so?

WILSON: Well, you see, Dr. Watson, I was pleased with my new source of income, but puzzled over why anyone should want me to copy out the encyclopedia. In fact, by nightfall I had almost convinced myself that it was all a great hoax.

HOLMES: Did it prove to be a great hoax?

WILSON: On the contrary. The next day, when I reported for work, there was the encyclopedia laid open upon the table, the page at letter "A." Mr. Duncan Ross was there, and he started me off, then left. At two o'clock he returned, complimented me upon the amount that I had written, bade me good day, and locked the door of his office after me.

HOLMES: How long did this procedure continue?

WILSON: This went on day after day, Mr. Holmes, and on Saturday, the manager came in and plunked down four golden sovereigns for my week's work. It was the same the next week, and the same the week after. Every morning I was there at ten, and every afternoon I left at two. Eight weeks passed away like this, and I had written about Abbots and Archery and Armour and Architecture and Attica, and hoped that with diligence I might get on to the B's before very long. It had cost me something for paper, but it was worth it. Then suddenly—

WATSON: Yes?

WILSON: The whole business came to an end.

HOLMES: To an end!

WILSON *(A bit puzzled):* Yes, sir. This very morning. I went to my work as usual at ten o'clock, but the door was shut and locked, with a little square of cardboard hammered onto the middle of the panel with a tack. Here it is, and you can read it for yourself.

HOLMES: Hm, how curious.

WATSON: What does it say, Holmes?

HOLMES: "The Red-Headed League is dissolved. June 22, 1890." (WATSON *laughs, and* HOLMES *joins in.)*

WILSON (*Indignantly*): I cannot see that there is anything very funny. If you can do nothing other than laugh at me, I can go elsewhere.

HOLMES: Oh, no, no, I shouldn't miss your case for the world. But you must admit that it has a slightly comical side to it. Pray, what steps did you take when you found this card on the door?

WILSON: I was staggered, sir. I did not know what to do. Then I called at the landlord's, and asked if he could tell me what had become of the Red-Headed League. He looked at me, astonished, and said . . .

LANDLORD (*Puzzled*): Red-Headed League, you say? I never heard of such a body.

WILSON: Well, then, can you tell me what happened to Mr. Duncan Ross?

LANDLORD: What happened to whom?

WILSON: Duncan Ross.

LANDLORD: Ross? I know of no one of that name.

WILSON: Well, then, what happened to the gentleman who rented number four?

LANDLORD: Oh, you mean the red-headed man. His name was William Morris. He was a solicitor and was using my room as a temporary convenience until his new premises were ready. He moved out yesterday.

WILSON: Where could I find him, sir?

LANDLORD: He's at his new offices. Let me see; he did tell me the address. What was it now? Ah, yes. 17 King Edward Street, near St. Paul's. . . .

HOLMES (*Muttering*): 17 King Edward Street. I'll make a note of that, Mr. Wilson. It may help us.

WILSON: Well, I already checked there, but there was no one there of either the name of William Morris *or* Duncan Ross. It was a manufacturer of artificial knee-caps. Well, at that, I knew not what to do, so decided to take the advice of my assistant, Spaulding, who said simply to wait. But I got impatient, sir, and hearing that Sherlock Holmes was very clever at such things, I decided to come here for aid.

HOLMES: And you did wisely, Mr. Wilson. From what you have said, I think it is possible that a far more serious issue may be at stake than might at first appear.

WILSON: The issue is quite serious enough as it is. I have lost four pounds a week!

HOLMES: Mr. Watson and I will do our best to help you, Mr. Wilson. But first, a few questions. This assistant of yours who first called your attention to the advertisement—how long has he been with you?

WILSON: He'd been with me about a month at that time. He answered an advertisement that I placed in the paper.

HOLMES: Was he the only applicant?

WILSON: No, I had a dozen.

HOLMES: Why did you pick him?

WILSON: Because he was intelligent and handy, and would come at half wages, in fact.

WATSON: What is he like, this Vincent Spaulding?

WILSON: Small, stout-built, very quick in his ways, no hair on his face—though he's not short of thirty. He has a white splash of acid upon his forehead.

HOLMES (*Excitedly*): Acid, you say? Yes, I thought as much. Have you ever observed that his ears are pierced for earrings?

WILSON: Yes, sir. He told me that a gypsy had done it for him when he was a lad.

HOLMES: Hm-m. He is still with you?

WILSON: Oh yes, sir; I have only just left him. But I must be on my way. Will there be anything else you require to ask of me, gentlemen?

WATSON: Not for my part, Wilson.

HOLMES: Yes, I have one more question. All the mornings that you were out—did your assistant attend to your business in your absence?

WILSON: Yes, sir, and he's honest and careful enough. Nothing to complain of, sir. There's never very much to do of a morning.

HOLMES: I believe you have given us all the information we shall need, Mr. Wilson. I shall be happy to give you an opinion on the subject in the course of a day or two. Today is Saturday, and I hope that by Monday we may come to a conclusion. Good day, Mr. Wilson.

WILSON: Good day, Dr. Watson, Mr. Holmes.

HOLMES *(After a pause):* Watson, what do you make of it all?

WATSON: I make nothing of it. It is a most mysterious business.

HOLMES: As a rule, the more bizarre a thing is, the less mysterious it proves to be. But we must be prompt over this matter.

WATSON: What are you going to do, then?

HOLMES: We are going to the pawnbroker's shop of Mr. Jabez Wilson.

WATSON: Whatever for?

HOLMES: To investigate, my dear Watson. To investigate!

NARRATOR: Holmes and Watson set out at once for Jabez Wilson's shop. After leaving their cab a short distance away, they stroll down the street.

HOLMES: There, Watson. See the three gilt balls? That is the place.

WATSON: Yes, Wilson's name is painted over the door. But now that you are here, what are you going to do?

HOLMES: First, an experiment.

NARRATOR: Holmes pounds his walking stick on the pavement.

Watson *(Taken aback):* Pounding your stick on the pavement?

HOLMES: And now, to knock on the door. I hope that Spaulding fellow answers.

SPAULDING: Won't you step in, gentlemen?

HOLMES: Thank you, but I only wished to ask you how one would go from here to the Strand.

SPAULDING: Oh. Third right, fourth left, sir. Good day.

HOLMES: Smart fellow, that. He is, in my judgment, the fourth smartest man in London, and for daring I am not sure that he has not a claim to be third. I have known something of him before.

WATSON: Evidently Mr. Wilson's assistant counts for a good deal in this mystery of the Red-Headed League. I am sure that you inquired your way merely that you might see him.

HOLMES: Not him. The knees of his trousers.

WATSON: And what did you see?

HOLMES: What I expected to see.

WATSON: Why did you beat the pavement before knocking on the door?

HOLMES: My dear doctor, this is a time for observation, not for talk. We are spies in an enemy's country. We know something of this city square. Let us now explore the parts which lie behind it.

NARRATOR: Holmes and Watson continue on down the street and around the block. Holmes observes carefully each building they pass.

HOLMES: Let me see. I should just like to remember the order of the houses here. There is the tobacconist's, the little newspaper shop, the Coburg branch of the City and Suburban Bank, the restaurant, and the carriage-builder's. That carries us right onto the other block, on which stands the pawnbroker's establishment of our friend, Jabez Wilson. This business of Wilson's is serious. A considerable crime is in contemplation. I have every reason to believe that we shall be in time to stop it. But today being Saturday rather complicates matters. I shall want your help tonight, Watson. Will you come to Baker Street at ten? Goodbye for now, then, Dr. Watson.

NARRATOR: Promptly at ten, Watson arrives at Baker Street, and he and Holmes take a carriage, and set off into the night. Watson questions Holmes about the adventure as the carriage drives them through the city . . .

WATSON: Will you not tell me, Holmes, where we are going, or whom we seek?

HOLMES: I shall gladly do both. We are now going to the Coburg branch of the City and Suburban Bank. The man we seek is none other than John Clay.

WATSON: John Clay! You mean the thief and forger who has escaped the police so many times?

HOLMES: The same, and you may add murderer to your list. His brain is as cunning as his fingers, and though we meet signs of him at every turn, we have never known where to meet the man.

WATSON: Why, all of London has been on his trail for years!

HOLMES: I hope that I may have the pleasure of introducing you to him tonight!

NARRATOR: Leaving the carriage some distance away, Holmes and Watson cautiously enter the bank with a key that Holmes produces without an explanation. They descend to the cellar . . .

HOLMES (Softly): Here, Watson. Through here. Righto!

WATSON (Quietly): Is this the cellar of the bank, then?

HOLMES: It is. We must act quickly, for time is of the essence. I perceive that the ceiling is thick enough. We are not vulnerable from above.

WATSON: Nor from below. The floor seems . . . why, dear me! A hollow sound!

HOLMES: I must really ask you to be a little more quiet. Sit down on one of those boxes while I shade the light.

WATSON: What is in these great packing-cases, Holmes?

HOLMES: The 30,000 napoleons of French gold from the Bank of France.

WATSON: What!

HOLMES: It has become known that this gold was being stored, completely packed, in the cellar where we now find ourselves. The directors of the bank began to have misgivings about leaving so large a quantity of gold about, and now it appears that their fears were well justified. The bank is to be robbed tonight, if I am not mistaken.

WATSON: How so? And only the two of us to stop the thieves?

HOLMES: I have ordered an inspector and two officers to be at the one possible retreat—the front door.

WATSON: How, then, will the thieves enter?

HOLMES: Through a hole in the floor.

WATSON: What!

HOLMES (Whispering): Huddle in the shadows! One of the stones is moving! They are coming. Hush!

NARRATOR: There is a chink of stones, and then Vincent Spaulding's voice is heard faintly, talking to another . . .

SPAULDING: It's all clear. Have you the chisel and the bags?

HOLMES *(Suddenly):* I have you, John Clay!

SPAULDING *(Calling out):* Run, Archie! I'm caught!

HOLMES: It's no use, John Clay. You have no chance at all. You did not reckon with Sherlock Holmes. It is no use!

SPAULDING: So I see. I fancy my friend has escaped though. At least my struggle with you gave him that chance. You are not totally successful.

WATSON: The door was guarded. There are three men waiting for him.

SPAULDING: Oh, indeed. You seem to have done the thing completely. I must compliment you.

HOLMES: And I you. Your red-headed idea was very clever.

WATSON: Ah, Clay, you'll be seeing your friend soon—in court, you scoundrel!

SPAULDING *(With dignity):* I beg your pardon. You may not be aware that John Clay has royal blood in his veins. Have the goodness when you address me always to say "sir" and "please."

HOLMES *(Laughing):* As you wish, John Clay. Well, would you please, sir, march upstairs, sir, where we can please to get a cab, sir, to carry Your Highness to the police station—sir?

NARRATOR: A short time later, back at Baker Street, Holmes explains to Watson . . .

HOLMES: It was obvious from the start that the purpose of the Red-Headed League was to get our friend, Jabez Wilson, out of the way for a few hours every day. The plot was suggested, I'm sure, by Wilson's own hair. The four pounds a week was a lure—and who could not afford four pounds who was gambling on thirty thousand? They put in the advertisement. One accomplice posed as Duncan Ross, the other insured that Wilson would apply. From the time I heard that the assistant had come for half wages, I knew he had some strange motive for securing the station.

WATSON: How could you guess what the motive was?

HOLMES: Wilson's business is very small. It must be, then, the house itself that was of value. When I thought of the assistant's fondness for photography and his vanishing constantly into the cellar, I realized at once that that was it.

WATSON: Yes, I remember now. Wilson mentioned that.

HOLMES: The description of the assistant convinced me that it was the notorious Clay himself. But what could he be doing in the cellar of a pawnbroker, I asked myself. Why, digging a tunnel, of course, each day over a period of months. Then I wondered, what building could he be tunneling into? Our visit to the actual scene itself showed me that. Remember I observed that the bank was right around the corner from Wilson's?

WATSON: Now that you mention it, I do indeed.

HOLMES: I surprised you, I recall, by tapping my

stick on the pavement. That was to determine whether the cellar extended to the front of the buildings. Then I paid a call on John Clay himself—at that time known to us as Spaulding, the assistant.

WATSON: Yes. You said you wanted to observe his knees. What did you see?

HOLMES: You yourself must have noticed how worn, wrinkled and stained they were—which was a natural consequence of his burrowing. All my conclusions assembled, I called Scotland Yard and the bank, and secured permission and a key for our admittance.

WATSON: How could you tell that they would make their attempt tonight?

HOLMES: When they closed their League offices, that was a sign that they cared no longer about Mr. Jabez Wilson's presence—in other words, that they had completed their tunnel. But it was essential that they should use it soon, as it might be discovered. Saturday would suit them best, as it would give them two days for their escape. For all these reasons I expected them to come tonight.

WATSON: Ah, you reasoned it out beautifully. It is so long a chain, and yet every link rings true. It was indeed remarkable, Sherlock Holmes. Remarkable.

HOLMES: On the contrary, it was elementary, my dear Watson. Elementary!

THE END

Thinking About It

Sherlock Holmes and the Red-Headed League

1. Mysteries are a favorite form of entertainment, whether in book, movie, or play form. In fact, some people say, "I love a mystery!" Do you? If so, why? If not, why not? What thoughts, pro or con, went through your mind as you read or heard *Sherlock Holmes and the Red-Headed League?*

2. Were you able to solve the mystery of the Red-Headed League before Sherlock Holmes explained it? When? What clues led you or him to the answer?

3. A mystery needs to be credible—that is, the audience needs to believe in it. What seven important suggestions do you have for producers of this play to help make their production credible?

Aïda

Story told by Leontyne Price
Illustrations by Leo and Diane Dillon

Long ago, in the faraway land of Ethiopia, there lived a princess named Aïda. She was as fair as the sunrise and gentle as starlight touching a flower. Her father, the great King Amonasro, loved her dearly.

It was a time of terrible fear and danger in Ethiopia, for the kingdom was at war with its neighbor, Egypt. Both countries raided each other's lands, killing or enslaving their enemies.

For the safety of his people, King Amonasro set strict boundaries at the borders of his country, and no Ethiopian was allowed beyond them.

The Princess Aïda was young and, locked within the palace, she grew restless. So, one morning, Aïda and her trusted friends disobeyed the King's command. They disguised themselves and slipped away from the palace guards.

It was a glorious day of freedom, out in the gentle breezes and lush green fields of their beautiful country. But Aïda wandered farther than she should have. Off on her own, enjoying the warm sun and fresh country air, she did not hear her friends in the distance when they shouted, "Aïda! Beware! Come back!"

Once again, Egyptian soldiers had invaded Ethiopia, crossing the south edge of the River Nile. Now they marched toward Aïda.

When she finally did hear her friends' warning, it was too late. Soldiers seized her. Bound with ropes and chains, Aïda, the Royal Princess of Ethiopia, was carried off to Egypt as a slave.

Aïda had learned her royal lessons well. She revealed to no one that she was the daughter of King Amonasro of Ethiopia. But her beauty and noble bearing attracted great attention. So sparkling and unusual was she that the all-powerful Pharaoh, the ruler of Egypt, chose her from among thousands of captured slaves to be his gift—a personal handmaiden—to his only daughter, the Princess Amneris.

It was easy for Aïda to perform the duties of a servant, for she remembered what her own handmaidens had done. The Egyptian Princess Amneris was fascinated, for Aïda was different from any slave she had ever seen. She wanted her new handmaiden to be her closest companion.

Even with the special privileges granted to one so close to the Royal Princess, Aïda felt nothing but despair. All her life she had been the beloved daughter of Ethiopia's King, and now she was a slave to her father's enemy. She knew there was no hope of seeing Ethiopia again.

There was one source of light in her life, however. For Radames, the handsome young captain of the Egyptian Army, had fallen in love with the gentle, beautiful slave the moment he saw her.

She, too, had fallen for Radames, despite his position as an enemy of her homeland.

They met often, in secret, by the Temple of Isis, and in the joy of their moments together, Radames confided his dreams to Aïda.

"I will lead the Egyptian Army to victory," he told her, "and when I return, our countries will be united, and you will become my bride and reign as the Queen of your people. It will not be long, I promise."

The day finally came when the Pharaoh was to hold court and announce the new leader of the war against Ethiopia.

Amid the majestic columns of a great hall in the palace, Egypt's High Priest, Ramfis, confided to Radames: "There are rumors that the Ethiopians plan to attack. Prepare yourself, for the Goddess Isis has chosen, and the great honor of leadership may be bestowed upon you."

All his life, Radames had dreamed of this day. If he became the new leader, he could return triumphant to free Aïda and marry her. "Ah, heavenly Aïda," he thought. "I could finally enthrone you in your native land."

Radames was deep in thought when Princess Amneris stepped from the shadows. She, too, was in love with the handsome leader, but she suspected he loved another.

Aïda suddenly appeared.

Oh, how Radames's eyes filled with passion! And when Amneris saw the look that passed between them, she was seized with suspicion and jealousy. Could Radames prefer a *slave* to the Princess of Egypt? It was intolerable! But her fury was interrupted by trumpets heralding the arrival of the Pharaoh.

A messenger came forward to give his report.

"Mighty Pharaoh, the Ethiopians have attacked. They are led by the fierce warrior King Amonasro, who has invaded Egypt!"

A thunder of anger broke out in court, and upon hearing her father's name, Aïda quietly cried out in fear.

The Pharaoh rose, and the crowd grew still.

"Radames will lead our army," he cried. "It is the decree of the Goddess Isis. Death to the Ethiopians! Victory to Egypt!" he shouted. "Return victorious, Radames!" he commanded.

"Return victorious! Return victorious!" the throng shouted, and Aïda, too, was stirred by the cry. In spite of herself, she also began to shout, "Return victorious! Return victorious!" as the court led the soldiers off to battle. Aïda was now left alone.

"Return victorious!" she called after Radames, but as her own voice echoed in the great hall, she suddenly realized she was asking for the death of her father, her mother, her friends, and all those she cherished. Yet how could she pray for the death of the man she loved?

Aïda was shocked. Her heart was torn between Radames and her loyalty to her father and Ethiopia. She fell to her knees and prayed.

"Oh, great gods of my youth!" she cried. "Pity me!"

That night, the halls of the temple rang as the priestesses chanted the sacred consecration song. The High Priest, Ramfis, led prayers to Phtha, the creator of life and mightiest Egyptian god, as he gave the great hero the sacred sword of Egypt.

"Let the sword of Radames be the strength of our nation! Let his bravery in battle crush the Ethiopians! Protect our land," they prayed, "and make Radames the most magnificent warrior of all."

"Praise to Phtha! Praise to Phtha!" the Egyptians chanted, and the priestesses danced a sacred dance to please the great god and ensure death to their enemies.

With Radames gone, time passed slowly for Aïda. But soon the prayers of the priests were granted. A special day dawned for Egypt—a day of ceremony and grandeur, of pomp and pageantry. The Ethiopians had been defeated at last.

Amneris sat before her mirror. Surrounded by slaves and adorned in her most beautiful gown and jewels, she was pleased with her reflection. Surely today when Radames returned, he would be struck by her radiance. Yet despite her vanity, she secretly burned with jealousy to think that Aïda, a mere handmaiden, might truly be loved by Radames.

So Amneris decided to test her privileged slave. And when gentle Aïda entered the royal chambers, Amneris sobbed, pretending great grief.

"Oh, Aïda, Aïda!" she cried in a shaking voice. "Egypt has lost its finest warrior. Radames has been killed in battle!"

Immediately Aïda wept with the pain of one whose heart has been broken forever. There was no longer any doubt in Amneris's mind.

"It is all a lie!" she shouted. "Radames was not killed. He lives!"

Aïda's tears of sorrow turned to tears of joy.

Overcome with fury, Amneris hurled Aïda to the floor. "How dare you, a lowly slave, love the same man loved by the Princess of Egypt?"

But Aïda, too, was a Princess. She rose proudly. She was about to tell Amneris the truth, but she stopped herself. Instead, with great difficulty, she asked to be forgiven.

"Have mercy on me," she begged. "Your power is unquestioned—you have all that a person could want. But what do I have to live for? My love of Radames, and that alone."

Aïda's plea only fueled Amneris's rage. She stormed out of the chamber, leaving Aïda to fear the worst.

Flags flew, and the entire city gathered to see the grand spectacle of the victory parade led by the Pharaoh, the Princess, and the High Priest. Trumpets blared, and dancing girls threw rose petals to form a welcoming carpet before the magnificent chariot of Radames.

The handsome warrior dismounted and knelt be-

fore the royal throne. When Amneris placed a laurel wreath on his head, the crowd was wild with joy.

"Hail to the conqueror!" they roared. "Hail to Radames!"

The Pharaoh proclaimed, "Radames, you are my greatest soldier. As a reward, whatever you wish shall be yours."

When Radames rose, he saw Aïda. Amneris saw the look of love on his face, and she was consumed with jealousy. Yet he dared not ask for Aïda's hand, not at that moment in public court.

"Mighty Pharaoh," he said instead, "I ask that you allow me to call forth our prisoners of war."

The Pharaoh granted Radames's request, and the Ethiopians were led into the square in chains. One tall, proud man stood out above the rest. Aïda gasped. It was her father!

The crowd was shocked to see her run and embrace him, but he whispered to her, "Do not betray that I am King."

Amonasro addressed the Pharaoh. "I am Aïda's father, and I have faithfully fought for my sovereign, who died in battle. I am prepared to die for him and my country, but I beseech you to have mercy on those who have been defeated."

With outstretched arms, Aïda joined the Ethiopians. "Let the prisoners go free," she begged Radames and the Pharaoh.

So moved by her appeal, the Egyptian people

joined in, and their cries urged the Pharaoh to allow the captured soldiers to be released.

"No!" the High Priest, Ramfis, cried. "The Ethiopians are still a threat and should be put to death."

"Their freedom is my wish," Radames told the Pharaoh.

"Unchain the Ethiopians!" the Pharaoh ordered. "But you, Aïda's father, must remain my prisoner as a pledge of your people's good faith."

An even greater reward was now to be bestowed upon Egypt's greatest warrior. The Pharaoh led Amneris to Radames.

"My daughter will be your bride," he proclaimed, joining their hands. "One day, you shall be Pharaoh, and together you will rule."

Radames was horrified. He dared not refuse the Pharaoh. He bowed and pretended gratitude, but his heart was filled with sorrow. Amneris looked scornfully at her handmaiden.

Aïda wept in her father's arms as the triumphant Egyptian Princess held Radames's hand and led him to the palace.

"Do not lose faith," Amonasro whispered to his daughter. "Ethiopia will soon avenge our conquerors."

It was the eve of the great wedding, and a full moon shone on the dark waters of the River Nile beside the Temple of Isis. By boat, the High Priest, Ramfis, brought Amneris to the Temple.

There she was to pray that her marriage be blessed. Little did she know that Radames had sent a message to Aïda, who was waiting to meet him nearby.

Aïda sadly watched the moonlit river and longed with all her heart and soul to return to her beloved homeland. Suddenly she heard Radames approach. But when the man came closer, she was stunned to see that it was her father, King Amonasro.

"Listen carefully, Aïda," he said sternly. "My plan will bring both you and Radames back to Ethiopia. Our soldiers stand ready to attack when I signal. There is a secret, unguarded road, but only Radames knows it. It is your duty as the Princess of Ethiopia to make him reveal this path."

"Father!" she cried, "I *cannot* betray Radames!"

With anger and disdain, King Amonasro forced her to her knees. "You are no longer my daughter! You are nothing more than a lowly slave of the Egyptians and a betrayer of your country! Have you forgotten your loved ones who were slaughtered without mercy by these, your enemies?"

"You are wrong! I am *not* and will *never* be a slave to anyone. I am the Princess of Ethiopia, and I have never forgotten my royal blood. My duty to you and to my country will always be first in my heart!"

Even as she swore to obey his command, she cried inside for what her father and her dear country would cost her. Amonasro embraced her to give her courage, and he hid in the bushes to listen.

When Radames finally came, he was breathless with love. But Aïda turned on him scornfully.

"How could you betray me and marry Amneris as your reward?"

"Aïda, you have always been my love. My passion for you is deeper than the Nile, deeper than life itself," Radames told her.

"Then show me," Aïda demanded. "You have betrayed me. And if you truly love me, you will leave Egypt tonight and flee with me to Ethiopia. Only there will we find happiness and peace."

Radames was torn. The thought of leaving Egypt was unbearable, but the thought of living without Aïda was even more painful. At last, after much persuasion, he agreed to flee.

"The roads are heavily guarded by your soldiers. How will we escape?" she asked.

"All the roads are guarded except one," he told her. "The Gorges of Napata."

"The Gorges of Napata!" a voice rang out. Amonasro sprang from his hiding place. He was ready to attack with his army.

Radames could not believe it. "You, Aïda's father, are King of Ethiopia?" He was overcome. "I have sacrificed my country for my love of you!" he cried to Aïda.

"Come with us now," Amonasro told Radames. "You and Aïda will reign happily in Ethiopia."

But as the King took Radames's hand to lead him away, a shout rang out in the darkness. "Traitor!"

It was Amneris. She and the High Priest had come from the temple and had overheard the plot.

"Traitor!" she screamed again.

Amonasro leapt to kill Amneris with his dagger, but Radames ran between to shield her.

"Go quickly!" he warned Aïda and Amonasro, and the King ran, dragging Aïda with him.

Radames stood before Amneris and the High Priest. He did not try to escape. Instead, he threw down his sword.

"I surrender!" he cried. "I am your prisoner!"

The treason of Radames shocked and infuriated all of Egypt. Guards locked him in the deepest dungeon in the palace. Soon his trial would begin, and he would be sentenced to a horrible death.

Amneris was in a state of grief. Her love for Radames had not diminished. Deep in her heart, she knew he had not meant to betray his country. Her own jealousy had made the mighty warrior a prisoner. She longed to beg her father, the Pharaoh, to release him, but she knew Radames still loved Aïda. She also knew soldiers had killed Amonasro, but Aïda had escaped and was still alive—somewhere.

In desperation, Amneris commanded the guards to bring Radames to her. She humbled herself and pleaded with him to forget Aïda.

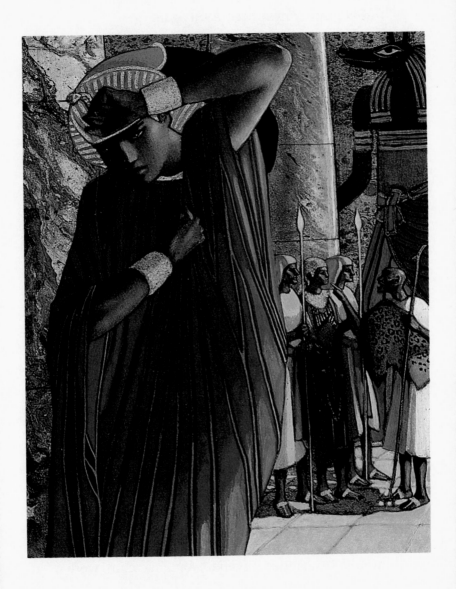

"I will find a way to set you free, free to marry me and share the throne of Egypt," she said. "But you must never see Aïda again."

Radames refused. "You are Princess of Egypt, my country; and you have all that anyone could ask for. Yet I will always love Aïda, and there will never be room in my heart for anyone else."

The more Amneris begged him, the more strongly he refused.

When the priests came to take Radames, Amneris was in a rage of anger and jealousy, and she made no attempt to stop them. But when he left, she fell to the ground in tears, cringing as she heard the priests loudly accuse Radames of betrayal.

"Traitor! Traitor!" the High Priest, Ramfis, shouted again and again, but Radames never uttered a word to defend himself. Louder and louder the cruel accusations were hurled at him.

Amneris prayed to Isis and the other gods of Egypt to show mercy and save the man she loved, but the gods were silent.

The tribunal of priests pronounced Radames guilty of treason and sentenced him to be buried alive.

As the priests passed from the trial, Amneris flung herself before the High Priest. She insulted him and threatened revenge, but her cries were in vain.

"Radames, the traitor, will die," he said coldly.

Only the priests and guards were allowed to watch Radames walk into the deepest vault below. They sealed the last opening, shutting out all light and the last breath of fresh air. Alone, waiting quietly for death, Radames thought only of Aïda. He would never see her sparkling eyes and gentle smile again.

Suddenly, in the darkness, he heard Aïda's voice. At first, Radames thought it was a dream. But no—she had escaped and was hiding in the vault, waiting for him.

"Aïda, my love, you are too young and too beautiful to die."

Radames pushed in vain, trying to open the vault.

But Aïda gently placed her arms around him. With a tender kiss, she told him to stop.

"Remember, we will never be separated again. For eternity, we will be together."

And with all the love in the world, they held each other close—so close—as if they would never part.

Above their tomb, dressed in black, Princess Amneris prayed to the gods to forgive her and to grant heavenly rest to Radames, her love.

The gods granted her wish, but not as she hoped. For as she prayed to the gods and wept, a peaceful death had come to the Ethiopian Princess Aïda and Radames, the greatest warrior of Egypt. Finally they were together—forever in each other's arms.

Storyteller's Note

Leontyne Price

Leontyne Price

Aïda as a heroine—and *Aïda* as an opera—has been meaningful, poignant, and personal for me. In many ways, I believe Aïda is a portrait of my inner self.

She was my best friend operatically and was a natural for me because my skin was my costume. This fact was a positive and strong feeling and allowed me a freedom of expression, of movement, and of interpretation that other operatic heroines I performed did not. I always felt, while performing Aïda, that I was expressing all of myself —as an American, as a woman, and as a human being.

Vocally, the role was perfectly suited to my voice in every respect—lyrically, dramatically, and in timbre. The role presented no difficulties, and because my voice was infused with the emotions I felt about Aïda, I sang with vocal ease and great enjoyment.

My first Grand Opera performance of this noble Ethiopian princess's story was on the stage of the War Memorial Opera House in San Francisco in 1957. Totally prepared, eager, and excited, I performed my debut Aïda with great success. I went on to perform Aïda at the Chicago Lyric Opera House, the Arena di Verona and La Scala in Italy, the Vienna Staatsoper, the Paris Opera House, Covent Garden in London, the Hamburg Staatsoper in Germany, and my home opera house, the Metropolitan Opera House in New York City—where I performed the role more often than in any other opera house.

Aïda has given me great inspiration on stage and off. Her deep devotion and love for her country and for her people—her nobility, strength, and courage—are all qualities I aspire to as a human being. I will never forget her.

Pulling It All Together

The First Magnificent Web

1. Aïda's loyalty to her father conflicted with her love for Radames. Think of a real situation or a movie in which someone's loyalties are in conflict. Describe the conflict and what happened.

2. Leo and Diane Dillon illustrated *Aïda* with acrylic paint on acetate and marbelized paper. Describe the illustrations and how they make you feel.

3. People tell stories as a way of entertaining each other. "Nothing to Be Afraid Of" is fun to read, as the play about Sherlock Holmes is fun to see performed. Using examples from this book, tell what makes a story entertaining.

Another Book About *Aïda*
The Complete Guide to Aïda by Rebecca Knaust gives details about *Aïda*—biographical background, staging, character descriptions, and best-known melodies—as well as interesting facts about Verdi.

Books to Enjoy

Everywhere
by Bruce Brooks
Harper, 1990

A young boy uses some outrageous tactics to help his new friend save his grandfather, who has suffered a stroke. Here is creative problem solving at its funniest.

In Your Own Words: A Beginner's Guide to Writing
by Sylvia Cassedy
Harper, 1990

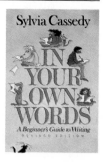

The world is full of fascinating experiences and details for you to put down on paper in your own special way. This book could be your guide to writing a story that becomes a bestseller!

Sing Me a Story
by Jane Rosenberg
Thames and Hudson, 1989

What's all that singing about? Here are the thrilling stories of fifteen great operas—stories about princesses, dragons, and lovers; stories that can make you laugh or cry, and pictures that make the stories come alive.

Sherlock Holmes: Selected Stories

by Diana Stewart, based on stories
by Arthur Conan Doyle
Raintree, 1980

Match wits with the master detective of Baker Street as he gathers clues and solves mysteries. You won't need a magnifying glass, but a sharp eye is essential.

The Knee-High Man and Other Tales

by Julius Lester
Dial, 1972

How can you get through life? Some people are tricksters, as you'll learn in this collection of stories that have their origins in Africa. Each of the six tales has survived through the years because it is a good story told with humor.

Favorite Greek Myths

by Mary Pope Osborne
Scholastic, 1989

You're on an ancient Greek island. How would you explain weather changes, spider webs, and rainbows? Find out how the Greeks supplied answers to these and other questions in this collection of stories.

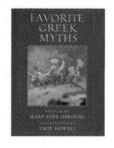

Literary Terms

Drama A drama, or play, is a story written to be acted. Dramas have characters, setting, and plot. Speeches are assigned to characters and interpreted by the actors. Stage directions tell actors how to interpret the lines and how to move around the stage. *Sherlock Holmes and the Red-Headed League* is a drama that is based on a well-known story.

Imagery Imagery is created by the words an author uses to help readers experience the way things look, sound, smell, taste, and feel. For example, in "The Invisible Beast," you experience the sounds of a heart "beating louder than a drum" and "footsteps falling."

Legend A legend is a story that has been handed down from the past. Legends often have some historical truth, and they may tell of a hero's great deeds. The story of *Aïda* is based on a legend about an Ethiopian princess.

Myth Myths are traditional stories that attempt to explain something about nature or the beliefs of a people. The myth about Arachne and Minerva tells why spiders weave marvelous webs.

Personification To personify an animal or object is to give it human qualities. In "Excursion," the conversation between the dancing bear and the flea is an example of personification. The fishes with bulging eyes who tell tales about fishermen in "Fish Story" is another example of personification.

Plot A plot is a series of events that make up a story. Often there is a cause-effect chain of events that brings about a change in a character. In the beginning of "Nothing to Be Afraid Of," Robin is a quiet child, not expected to give any trouble, but by the conclusion, after Anthea has introduced him to some frightening ideas, he is a very different child.

Point of view Point of view refers to the author's choice of narrator, or speaker. The narrator may be an observer of the action, as in "Nothing to Be Afraid Of" and "The Wish." Both stories are told from the third-person point of view in which the narrator tells who the characters are, what they do, and often what they are thinking, as well. Words like *he, she, it, they,* and *the child* are found with the third-person point of view.

Rhyme When two or more words have the same last, or ending, sounds, they are said to rhyme. In poetry, the last words in lines often rhyme, such as the words *stood* and *wood* in "Jabberwocky." This poem also includes rhyming words within lines— for example, *jaws* and *claws* in the line "The jaws that bite, the claws that catch!"

Short story A short story generally describes just one event and includes the story elements of characterization, setting, theme, and plot. The plot is simpler than that of a novel, perhaps describing just one event or a short series of events tightly woven together. "Nothing to Be Afraid Of" and "The Wish" are examples of short stories.

Glossary

Vocabulary from your selections

ac com plice (ə kom′plis), *n.* person who knowingly aids another in committing a crime or other wrong act.
ac cus tomed (ə kus′təmd), *adj.* **1** usual; customary. **2 accustomed to,** used to; in the habit of.

ban is ter (ban′ə stər), *n.* **1** Often, **banisters,** *pl.* balustrade of a staircase. **2** railing of a staircase.
be tray (bi trā′), *v.t.* **1** place in the hands of an enemy by treachery or disloyalty: *The fort was betrayed by its commander.* **2** be disloyal to (one's cause or leader); be unfaithful to. **3** disclose or reveal (secrets entrusted to one): *betray a friend's confidence.* —**be tray′er,** *n.*
bi zarre (bə zär′), *adj.* strikingly odd in appearance or style; fantastic; grotesque.

crane (def. *n* and 1)

chal lenge (chal′ənj), *v.,* **-lenged, -leng ing,** *n.* —*v.t.* **1** call to a game or contest. **2** call in question; doubt; dispute: *I challenge your statement; you must prove it before I believe it.* —*n.* **1** a call to a game or contest: *a challenge to a game of chess.* **2** a demand for proof of the truth of a statement; a doubting or questioning of the truth of a statement. **3** anything that claims or commands effort, interest, feeling, etc.
cher ish (cher′ish), *v.t.* hold dear; treat with affection; care for tenderly: *Parents cherish their children.*
com pel (kəm pel′), *v.t.,* **-pelled, -pel ling.** **1** drive or urge with force; force: *Rain compelled them to stop.* **2** cause or get by force.
con ceit (kən sēt′), *n.* too high an opinion of oneself or of one's ability, importance, etc.; vanity.
crane (krān), *n., v.,* **craned, cran ing.** —*n.* machine with a long, swinging arm, for lifting and moving heavy weights. —*v.t.* **1** move by, or as if by, a crane. **2** stretch (the neck) as a crane does, in order to see better. —**crane′like′,** *adj.*

de fi ance (di fī′əns), *n.* a defying; standing up against authority and refusing to recognize or obey it.
de fi ant (di fī′ənt), *adj.* showing defiance; openly resisting. —**de fi′ant ly,** *adv.*
dis solve (di zolv′), *v.,* **-solved, -solv ing.** —*v.t., v.i.* **1** change from a solid or gas to a liquid: *The warm air dissolved the ice.* **2** break up; end: *dissolve a partnership.* **3** fade away: *The dream dissolved when she woke up.*
dod der (dod′ər), *v.i.* be unsteady; tremble or shake from frailty. —**dod′der er,** *n.*

eld er (el′dər), *adj.* **1** born, produced, or formed before something else; older; senior: *my elder sister.* **2** prior in rank, validity, etc. —*n.* **1** Usually, **elders,** *pl.* person who is older than oneself; one's senior. **2** person of advanced years. **3** one of the older men of a tribe or community to whom age and experience have brought wisdom and judgment. [Old English *eldra,* comparative of *eald* old]

em bel lish (em bel′ish), *v.t.* **1** add beauty to; decorate; adorn; ornament. **2** make more interesting by adding real or imaginary details; elaborate: *embellish a story.* —**em bel′lish ment,** *n.*

en rage (en rāj′), *v.t.,* **-raged, -rag ing.** make very angry; make furious.

en throne (en thrōn′), *v.t.,* **-throned, -thron ing. 1** set on a throne. **2** place highest of all; exalt.

e ter ni ty (i tėr′nə tē), *n., pl.* **-ties. 1** all time; all the past and all the future; time without beginning or ending. **2** the endless period after death.

ex ag ge rate (eg zaj′ə rāt′), *v.,* **-rat ed, -rat ing.** —*v.t.* **1** make (something) greater than it is; overstate. **2** increase or enlarge abnormally. —*v.i.* say or think something is greater than it is; go beyond the truth: *He always exaggerates when he tells about things he has done.* [< Latin *exaggeratum* heaped up < *ex-* up + *agger* to heap]

ex ag ge ra tion (eg zaj′ə rā′shən), *n.* **1** an exaggerated statement; overstatement. **2** an exaggerating.

forge (fôrj, fōrj), *n., v.,* **forged, forg ing.** —*n.* an open fireplace or hearth with a bellows attached, used for heating metal very hot to be hammered into shape. —*v.t.* **1** shape (metal) by heating in a forge and then hammering. **2** make, shape, or form. **3** make or write (something false) to deceive; counterfeit: *forge a passport.* **4** sign (another's name) falsely to deceive. —*v.i.* **1** work at a forge. **2** commit forgery. —**forg′er,** *n.*

gouge (gouj), *n., v.,* **gouged, goug ing.** —*n.* **1** chisel with a curved, hollow blade, used for cutting round grooves or holes in wood. **2** groove or hole made by gouging. **3** INFORMAL. trick; cheat; swindle. —*v.t.* **1** cut with a gouge. **2** dig out; tear out.

han dle (han′dl), *n., v.,* **-dled, -dling.** —*n.* **1** a part of a thing made to be held or grasped by the hand. **2** SLANG. title or name. —*v.t.* **1** touch, feel, hold, or move with the hand; use the hands on.

hand maid en (hand′mād′n), *n.* **1** a female servant or attendant. **2** person or thing that serves.

heave (hēv), *v.,* **heaved** or **hove, heav ing.** —*v.t.* lift with force or effort; hoist: *She heaved the heavy box into the station wagon.* —*v.i.* **1** pull with force or effort; haul. **2** rise and fall alternately: *The waves heaved in the storm.* **3** breathe hard; pant; gasp. **4** be raised, thrown, or forced up; rise; swell; bulge: *The ground heaved from the earthquake.* [Old English *hebban*] —**heav′er,** *n.*

in so lence (in′sə ləns), *n.* bold rudeness; insulting behavior or speech.

in tol er a ble (in tol′ər ə bəl), *adj.* too much to be endured; unbearable: *intolerable pain.*

a hat	oi oil
ā age	ou out
ä far	u cup
e let	u̇ put
ē equal	ü rule
ėr term	
i it	ch child
ī ice	ng long
o hot	sh she
ō open	th thin
ô order	ᴛʜ then
	zh measure

ə = { a in about
e in taken
i in pencil
o in lemon
u in circus

< = derived from

forge (def. *n* and 1)

keen (kēn), *adj.* **1** so shaped as to cut well: *a keen blade.* **2** sharp; piercing; cutting. **3** strong; vivid: *keen competition.* **4** highly sensitive; able to perceive well; acute: *a keen mind.*

lamprey

lam prey (lam/prē), *n., pl.* **-preys.** any of an order of marine and freshwater vertebrate animals having a body like an eel, gill slits like a fish, no jaws, and a large, round mouth.

league (lēg), *n.* a union of persons, parties, or countries formed to help one another.

mis sion ar y (mish/ə ner/ē), *n., pl.* **-ar ies, 1** person sent on a religious mission. **2** person who works to advance some cause or idea.

Nic a ra gua (nik/ə rä/gwə), *n.* country in Central America, north of Costa Rica. 2,485,000 pop.; 57,100 sq. mi. (147,900 sq. km.) *Capital:* Managua. —**Nic/a ra/guan,** *adj., n.*

nymph (nimf), *n.* (in Greek and Roman myths) one of the lesser goddesses of nature, who lived in seas, rivers, fountains, springs, hills, woods, or trees.

old-tim er (ōld/tī/mər), *n.* INFORMAL. person who has long been a resident, member, worker, etc.

pawn bro ker (pôn/brō/kər), *n.* person who lends money at interest on articles that are left as security for the loan.

peas ant (pez/nt), *n.* **1** farmer of the working class in Europe. **2** any farm laborer of low social status. —*adj.* of peasants: *peasant labor.*

pe cul iar (pi kyü/lyər), *adj.* **1** out of the ordinary; strange; odd; unusual. **2** belonging to one area, person, or thing and not to another; special; particular; distinctive.

pen sion er (pen/shə nər), *n.* **1** person who receives a pension. **2** a hireling; dependent.

pine (pīn), *v.i.,* **pined, pin ing. 1** long eagerly; yearn: *pine for home.* **2** waste away with pain, hunger, grief, or desire: *pine with homesickness.*

plod (plod), *v.,* **plod ded, plod ding.** —*v.i.* **1** walk heavily or slowly; trudge. **2** proceed in a slow or dull way; work patiently with effort. —*v.t.* walk heavily or slowly along or through.

plough (plou), *n., v.t., v.i.* plow.

pon der (pon/dər), *v.t.* consider carefully; think over.

prime[1] (prīm), *adj.* first in rank or importance; chief; principal.

prime[2] (prīm), *n.* the best time, stage, or state: *be in the prime of life.* **2** the best part.

prime[3] (prīm), *v.t.,* **primed, prim ing. 1** prepare by putting something in or on. **2** pour water into (a pump) to start action.

pro ces sion (prə sesh/ən), *n.* something that moves forward; persons marching or riding: *a funeral procession.*

re cord (*v.* ri kôrd/; *n.* rek/ərd), *v.t.* **1** set down in writing so as to keep for future use: *record the proceedings at a meeting.* **2** put in some permanent form; keep for remembrance. —*n.* anything written and kept.

scoun drel (skoun′drəl), *n.* a wicked person without honor or good principles; villain; rascal.

sin gu lar (sing′gyə lər), *adj.* **1** extraordinary; unusual: *a person of singular ability, a story of singular interest.* **2** strange; odd; peculiar: *The detectives were greatly puzzled by the singular nature of the crime.* **3** being the only one of its kind: *an event singular in history.*

sov er eign (sov′rən), *n.* **1** supreme ruler; king or queen; monarch. **2** person, group, or nation having supreme control or dominion; master.

sprawl (sprôl), *v.i.* **1** toss or spread the arms and legs about, as an infant or animal lying on its back. **2** spread out in an irregular or awkward manner, as vines, handwriting, etc. **3** move awkwardly; scramble.

spring (spring), *v.,* **sprang** or **sprung, sprung, springing,** *n.* —*v.i.* **1** rise or move suddenly and lightly; leap; jump: *spring to attention.* **2** fly back or away as if by elastic force: *The branch sprang up when I dropped from it.* **3** come from some source; arise; grow. **4** begin to move, act, grow, appear, etc., suddenly; burst forth. —*v.t.* **1** cause to spring; cause to act by a spring: *spring a trap.* **2** bring out, produce, or make suddenly: *spring a surprise on someone.*
—*n.* leap or jump; bound: *a spring over the fence.*

squelch (skwelch), *v.t.* **1** cause to be silent; crush: *She squelched him with a look of contempt.* **2** strike or press on with crushing force; put down; squash; suppress. —*v.i.* walk in mud, water, wet shoes, etc., making a splashing sound; slosh.

steep (stēp), *v.i.* undergo soaking; soak: *Let the tea steep in boiling water for five minutes.* —*v.t.* **1** permit (something) to steep. **2** make thoroughly wet; saturate.

stump (stump), *n.* **1** the lower end of a tree or plant, left after the main part is broken or cut off. **2** a heavy step. **3** sound made by stiff walking or heavy steps; clump. —*v.i.* walk in a stiff, clumsy, or noisy way.

trag e dy (traj′ə dē), *n., pl.* **-dies.** **1** a serious play having an unhappy or disastrous ending. **2** a very sad or terrible happening.

trai tor (trā′tər), *n.* **1** person who betrays his or her country or ruler. **2** person who betrays a trust, duty, friend, etc.

trea son (trē′zn), *n.* **1** betrayal of one's country or ruler. **2** betrayal of a trust, duty, friend, etc.; treachery.

tre men dous (tri men′dəs), *adj.* **1** very severe; dreadful; awful: *a tremendous defeat.* **2** INFORMAL. very great; enormous: *a tremendous house.*

troll (trōl), *n.* (in Scandinavian folklore) an ugly dwarf or giant with supernatural powers, living underground or in caves.

venge ful (venj′fəl), *adj.* feeling or showing a strong desire for vengeance; vindictive.

wind y (win′dē), *adj.,* **wind i er, wind i est.** **1** having much wind: *a windy day.* **2** made of wind; empty: *windy talk.* **3** talking a great deal; voluble.

a	hat	oi	oil
ā	age	ou	out
ä	far	u	cup
e	let	u̇	put
ē	equal	ü	rule
ėr	term		
i	it	ch	child
ī	ice	ng	long
o	hot	sh	she
ō	open	th	thin
ô	order	ᴛʜ	then
		zh	measure

$$\mathbf{\theta} = \begin{cases} \text{a in about} \\ \text{e in taken} \\ \text{i in pencil} \\ \text{o in lemon} \\ \text{u in circus} \end{cases}$$

< = derived from

sovereign (def. 1)

Acknowledgments

Text

Page 6: "Nothing to Be Afraid Of" from *Nothing to Be Afraid Of* by Jan Mark. Copyright © 1980, 1981 by Jan Mark. Reprinted by permission of HarperCollins Publishers and Penguin Books Ltd.

Page 20: "The Invisible Beast" from *The Headless Horseman Rides Tonight* by Jack Prelutsky, illustrated by Arnold Lobel. Text copyright © 1980 by Jack Prelutsky. Illustrations copyright © 1980 by Arnold Lobel. Reprinted by permission of the Publisher, Greenwillow Books, a Division of William Morrow & Company, Inc.

Page 22: "Jabberwocky" by Lewis Carroll. *Through the Looking Glass,* 1871.

Page 24: "The Wish" from *Someone Like You* by Roald Dahl. Copyright 1953 by Roald Dahl. Reprinted by permission of Alfred A. Knopf, Inc.

Page 32: "American Weather" reprinted by permission of The Putnam Publishing Group from *On the Road with Charles Kuralt* by Charles Kuralt. Copyright © 1985 by CBS Inc.

Page 44: "Fish Story" from *Light Armour* by Richard Armour. Copyright 1954 by Richard Armour. Reprinted by permission of Kathleen S. Armour.

Page 45: "Excursion" from *Fresh Paint* by Eve Merriam. Copyright © 1986 by Eve Merriam. Reprinted by permission of Marian Reiner for the author.

Page 46: "The Weaving Contest" from *Favorite Greek Myths* retold by Mary Pope Osborne. Illustrated by Troy Howell. Text copyright © 1989 by Mary Pope Osborne. Illustrations copyright © 1989 by Troy Howell. All rights reserved. Reprinted by permission of Scholastic, Inc.

Page 52: *The Invisible Hunters* reprinted by permission of GRM Associates, Inc., Agents for Children's Book Press from the book *The Invisible Hunters* by Harriet Rohmer. Text copyright © 1987 by Harriet Rohmer. Illustrations copyright © 1987 by Joe Sam.

Page 61: "About the Story," by Harriet Rohmer. Copyright © 1991 by Harriet Rohmer.

Page 64: "About Earth Happenings" from *Earthmaker's Tales* by Gretchen Will Mayo. Copyright © 1989 by Gretchen Will Mayo. Reprinted with permission from Walker and Company.

Page 66: "Big Elk Digs Up the Mountains" from *Earthmaker's Tales* by Gretchen Will Mayo. Copyright © 1989 by Gretchen Will Mayo. Reprinted with permission from Walker and Company.

Page 74: "Sherlock Holmes and the Red-Headed League" by A. Conan Doyle, adapted by Lewy Olfson from *Popular Plays for Classroom Reading* edited by A. S. Burack and B. Alice Crossley. Copyright © 1974 by Plays, Inc. Reprinted by permission of Plays, Inc.

Page 98: *Aïda* as told by Leontyne Price. Copyright © 1990 by Leontyne Price, illustrations copyright © 1990 by Leo and Diane Dillon. Reprinted by permission of Harcourt Brace Jovanovich, Inc.

Page 117: "Storyteller's Note," by Leontyne Price. Copyright © 1990 by Leontyne Price. Reprinted by permission of Harcourt Brace Jovanovich, Inc.

Artists

Michael Paraskevas, Cover, 3, 4, 5, 6, 13, 19
Arnold Lobel, 20
Hal Mayforth, 23, 44, 45
Douglas Smith, 24, 28, 31
Troy Howell, 46, 49, 51
Joe Sam, 52, 56, 59, 63
Gretchen Will Mayo, 65, 66, 70, 73
Tim O'Brien, 74, 77, 82, 84, 87, 90, 93, 97
Leo and Diane Dillon, 98, 103, 106, 111, 113, 115

Photographs

Page 32 (top): Kazuhiko Nakano/Photonica
Page 32 (center): Mitsugu Hara/Photonica
Page 32 (bottom): Kazu Kuroki/Photonica
Page 35 (top): Harumi Koyano/Photonica
Page 35 (center & bottom): Yoshio Otsuka/Photonica
Page 38 (top): Mariko Abe/Photonica
Page 38 (center): Harumi Koyano/Photonica
Page 38 (bottom): Ken/Photonica
Page 43: Masano Kawana/Photonica
Page 61: Courtesy of Mary Dryovage
Page 117: James Heffernan

Glossary

The contents of the Glossary entries in this book have been adapted from *Advanced Dictionary,* Copyright © 1988, Scott, Foresman and Company.
Page 126: Breck P. Kent/ANIMALS ANIMALS
Page 127: Reg Wilson, London
Unless otherwise acknowledged, all photographs are the property of ScottForesman.

Illustrations owned and copyrighted by the illustrator.